THE HR HANDBOOK

A Practical Guide to Employee Experience

By Lee Nallalingham

Contents

Introduction

Employee experience can often be dismissed as a fluffy topic. Just the term 'employee experience' can conjure up images of employees lazing around in bean bag chairs or playing pool. It leads many, both in HR and Business Leadership, to often consider employee experience as a nice to have as opposed to a business essential. But let's be clear; employee experience is a business essential. Do you want to know why? Businesses with high levels of employee engagement make two and a half times more money than businesses without. Let me say that again just so that you are clear. Businesses that look after their people make two and a half times more money than businesses that do not. This is why employee experience has become one of the hottest trends in both HR and Business as a whole. It is not a nice to have; it is the key to building and sustaining a successful business.

So, how does employee experience enable businesses to consistently outperform? Simply put, the better the employee experience, the more engaged employees are. The more engaged employees are, the more productive they are. The more productive the employees are, the better the business results will be. This is kind of stating the obvious, but you will be amazed at how few organisations successfully connect these dots, which is why employee experience is often considered a nice to have rather than a business essential. But let's look at the facts. Research has consistently shown the benefits of employee engagement for several decades. For example, businesses in the top 20% for employee engagement scores see, on average, 41% less absenteeism from staff and 59% less turnover. Happy and engaged employees turn up for work more often and want to do their best. In addition, it's been found that employees that feel their voice is heard are 4.6 times more likely to perform their best. Therefore, organisations that empower their staff and ensure communication goes two ways as opposed to top-down, significantly outperform others. Furthermore, 89% of staff at companies that support wellbeing are more likely to recommend their employer as a great place to work.

So, ensuring that your organisation prioritises employee experience and engagement should be considered a business essential. If you want to have a successful business, it is an absolute no-brainer to look after your people. Why would you not want happy employees who are more productive and stay with the organisation for longer? Despite this, the state of employee experience and engagement within the corporate world isn't great. As a general rule, you should be aiming for an engagement score of 80% as a minimum. This means that 8 out of every 10 of your employees are happy and engaged. It is going to be rare to keep all of your employees happy, but you should be able to keep 80% of them happy. This is also in line with various pieces of research. For example, a general rule for hiring is that at any given time, about 20% of a talent pool is actively looking for a new role. Likewise, the average Glassdoor rating when aggregating all 100+ million employee reviews of their companies is 4 out of 5 stars. The best organisations score in excess of 90%, but if we are honest, many can only dream of getting to 80% and being 'average'. So, why is there such a disconnect between the obvious benefits of employee experience and engagement and the actual day-to-day reality within organisations?

The truth is that it is not easy to build and sustain an employee-centric culture because it involves doing a lot more than the bare minimum. In a world of competing priorities, organisations are consistently guilty of looking for the quick fix rather than putting in the work required to change organisational culture. It is often seen as easier to simply offer a member of staff a bit more money than to fix a toxic culture. But here is the truth, you can pay someone the best salary in the world, but if the environment is toxic, they are still going to leave. The irony is that research has consistently proven that you only need to pay someone an average salary and combine this with some meaningful work and a pleasant working environment, and they will be happy. So, in order to create an employee-centric culture that enables successful business outcomes, you need to do a lot more than just simply offering someone a salary.

The hard work needs to start with the quality of managers within the organisation. The old saying that people leave managers, not companies, is true. It has been proven to be true time and time again. The root cause of the overwhelming majority of attrition and disengagement is down to the manager. In fact, 70% of the variance in engagement scores can be directly attributed to the conduct of an employee's line manager. This is one of the biggest hurdles to an organisation building a winning environment. As an HR team, you could put in place the best people-centric policies in the world, but if you have a manager who treats their people like crap with no consequences, then the employee experience is not going to reflect the quality of the policies. This is why employee experience and engagement are inconsistent within an organisation and also why you will often hear a senior leader say that the feedback they receive in the annual engagement survey doesn't reflect their views. They might be treating their direct reports very well, but it doesn't change the fact that a middle manager 3 levels below them treats their team terribly.

As I share in my end-to-end management book, *The Manager Handbook: A Practical Guide to Managing Your Team*, the truth is that the majority of managers receive very little training or support. Organisations simply promote whoever the best individual contributor is to become a manager, regardless of whether or not they display any management capability. Promotions are essentially a reward for performing the last job well, not based on a person's ability to perform the next job well. Just because someone is a great accountant or software developer, this doesn't mean they are going to be good at managing other accountants or software developers. In fact, the traits that make someone a successful individual contributor are often the opposite of what would make someone a good people manager. This is backed up by research as well. It has been shown that up to 90% of first-time managers have little or no management capability at all. Those same managers are then just expected to know how to manage with very little support provided to help them make the right decisions. This is why 87% of managers state they wish they had been provided with more training and support when it comes to day-to-day people management issues. Sure, they know how to deliver the work required, but they don't know what to do when a member of staff has a close family member die two days before an important project deadline. Are they supposed to make the employee work to ensure the deadline is met, or let them take time to grieve and risk missing the deadline? This lack of support to set managers up for success has a huge impact on engagement and experience.

The fail-safe mechanism that can be used to catch these management issues and allow the organisation to remedy them is also rarely used correctly. This mechanism is the employee engagement survey. Employees consistently highlight the issues in their respective teams year after year, yet organisations rarely act on the feedback, and if they do, it is superficial. They will try to offer a few folks more money instead of asking the hard questions about why the same team seem to be raising the same issues every year. There are no consequences for the manager of the team despite consistent low engagement and high attrition within their team. Instead, at best, the company usually highlights the engagement scores at a town hall or in a companywide email and claims they have taken on board the feedback. They then announce some superficial changes before quietly reverting back to business as usual a couple of months later.

They then wonder why engagement continues to be low and why attrition continues to be high. This leads them to further de-prioritise employee experience and engagement initiatives because the spike in attrition combined with low productivity from a disengaged workforce puts business results at risk. So, rather than tackle the root cause of employee disengagement, the company will instead prioritise the business results. This leads to huge pressure on middle managers to have their team deliver. So, the poorly trained and supported middle managers 'crack the whip' and come down hard on the employees to do more, leading to even more disengagement and attrition. It is a vicious cycle playing out time and time again, and the outcomes have been seen in events such as 'The Great Resignation', where staff are no longer accepting such treatment and resigning in record numbers.

It is no surprise that employees are making this decision in many instances because it is clear their organisation is not listening to them and often has no intention of acting on the feedback they are provided. The organisation is communicating quite clearly to the staff that they are not important, and their opinions are not valued. After all, if an organisation asks for their views about what is and isn't working—how else would you expect an employee to feel when all of their feedback is ignored and not acted on. This is also why many companies struggle to get staff to complete the annual engagement survey. The belief among much of the working population is that the survey is pointless because no one will listen anyway.

There is an easy solution to this problem. Ultimately, one of the biggest challenges to executing on the work required is capacity. After all, in organisations with engagement and attrition issues, this always has a knock-on effect on business results, and so this is prioritised by management. This doesn't leave them with a huge amount of time to focus on anything else, even though the root cause of the poor results is because the team are disengaged. One of the easiest ways to combat this would be to include the people in the organisation in solving the problems. For example, if management conduct is consistently highlighted as an issue and the company can't afford to bring in experts to coach managers, have the internal team run a series of sharing sessions on good management techniques. You could have a junior member of staff share daily lessons via email of quotes on people management. You could have someone else send the management group a weekly list of management podcasts or YouTube channels. There are so many things that could be done by asking the organisation as a whole to help instead of centralising the responsibility to resolve the problems highlighted with a small group of senior leaders. If the complaint is around a lack of inclusion and diversity, ask your people to help set up internal groups to provide support and come up with ways to bring attention to specific issues.

Alas, this rarely happens, and so the problems persist, and staff end up leaving. The organisation will usually make some sort of last-ditch attempt to change their mind, and when this is turned down, they will conduct an exit interview. Exit interviews are, of course, a well-established practice, but very few organisations have considered the concept of a stay interview. Exit interviews can be useful, but they won't help you to keep an employee who has already decided to leave. Likewise, as much as the feedback from employee engagement surveys is often ignored, so too is the feedback from the exit interviews. It would be much more productive for an organisation to proactively have stay interviews with employees. A stay interview is a conversation between a manager and an employee to understand what is important to an employee. The conversation must be open, and the manager needs to put their ego to one side and allow the employee to talk candidly about their experience. By understanding what works and what doesn't, you can then focus on what keeps an employee motivated and engaged. As opposed to only address a problem once it has become severe enough that the person decides they need to leave. Sadly, this rarely happens, and research shows that roughly half of employees do not even have basic performance conversations with their manager on a quarterly basis.

It would, of course, be silly of me to claim this kind of experience is entirely accurate for every employee with every organisation, but most employees can relate to this kind of negative employee experience on some level. They will have experienced most of these things in some shape or form during the course of their career—sometimes all with one company and sometimes bits and pieces with different organisations. Some organisations create all of these negative touchpoints and many more; others only have a few of them. But either way, it is possible for your organisation to deliver an outstanding employee experience and often with very little need for a huge additional budget. In this book, I will share with you how I have personally built teams and processes that have delivered exceptional employee experience. This has led to teams that have seen attrition drop to as low as 4% from well over 50% (sometimes close to 100%!) and led to businesses that were losing money delivering record results. In addition to my own hands-on experience leading teams and processes, I will also share how I have advised over 100 multinational companies spanning 6 continents and 70+ countries on improving their own employee experience.

Chapter 1: The Role of HR

In this day and age, it is impossible to get away from the topic of 'The Future of . . .'—it is everywhere. As we navigate the fourth industrial revolution and the world of digital-first organisations seeming to disrupt everything with some sort of technology—HR has never been more important. The combination of businesses being disrupted, ways of working transforming even before we had heard of COVID-19, and a global talent shortage, people-related issues are at the top of most CEOs' priorities. The questions they ask are related to being able to attract, hire and retain top talent. They want to know how to retrain existing teams to ensure they have the right people not just to survive digital disruption but also to thrive as a result of it. This is the time for Human Resources to shine. The challenge for HR is that they also have to transform and pivot to meet the needs of businesses in current times. Just as businesses need to shake off the shackles of how things have always been done, so too do HR. So, what does the HR team need to do in order to meet the challenges both current and future?

The biggest shift Human Resources teams are going to have to undertake is in how they see their overall purpose within the organisation. This is most commonly discussed as a shift from an administrative function to a more strategic function, but this positioning often confuses traditional HR teams as they are unsure of what a strategic function involves. So, instead, I prefer to position this shift as one which requires the HR team to move from managing and facilitating various processes to one in which they deliver specific people-related outcomes. There is very little value add provided by traditional HR teams that are merely managing processes. These tasks are, of course, important, but to a large extent, they can now be managed more efficiently via either technology or outsourced vendors. Things such as tracking annual leave, processing payroll, or managing employment contracts should not be the core focus of a team. An example I share in my book *The Talent Acquisition Handbook: A Practical Guide to Candidate Experience* involves the talent acquisition team pivoting their focus. Rather than focusing their time on scheduling interviews, preparing employment contracts, and updating and posting job descriptions, they shift to higher value activities. This means that rather than managing the process, they take on responsibility for building the organisational employer brand to ensure talent pipelines are full. The team would also shift to coaching and advising leaders on what the external talent pool looks like, helping to shape internal decision-making on the type of talent to hire, how to structure teams, which markets to target, and so on.

In addition, the rewards team shouldn't be solely focused on updating the benchmarks and ensuring everyone falls into a relevant compa ratio. The team should instead be focused on creating new reward programmes that enable the organisation to differentiate themselves and outmanoeuvre competitors to ensure pay and benefits are attractive. This doesn't simply mean paying people a higher basic salary (this is rarely an option) but instead creating other ways to lock in great talent. For example, perhaps they want to create some sort of incentive allowing staff to keep a proportion of cost savings if they are able to improve a system or process and, at the same time, reduce cost. This would help create a culture of high performance and reward employees for creating value rather than simply performing tasks. Or it could mean things like more annual leave, better healthcare, a 4-day work week, etc. Likewise, the talent management and learning and development teams would be responsible for creating programmes that ensure the organisation is not entirely dependent on consistently hiring external talent to plug gaps. They would instead take on responsibility for outcomes such as ensuring a large percentage of open positions are filled by internal applicants, allowing the organisation to build its own capability. This same type of shift would take place across the rest of the HR team as well. All of this will lead to an HR team that is proactively solving people challenges, devising strategy, systems, and programs to help the organisation deliver on the overall business objectives as opposed to simply following processes and policies. With the right tools and strategy, it is possible to only require one HR professional per 100–150 employees and have none of them spend more than 10% of their time on any process-related activities.

This shift to owning outcomes and being able to directly impact strategy has another big benefit to HR teams. Not only will they be able to demonstrate the importance and value of the HR department, but HR teams will also be able to back this up with financial metrics. The HR department has long been one of the most important departments in an organisation. Anyone that thinks hiring, training, developing, and retaining isn't crucial to a business is deluded and should never be allowed near a leadership role. But HR teams have long struggled to demonstrate how their seemingly administrative activities impact the bottom line or how the department contributes to the organisational objectives. After all, it is often the management that are seen to be making the decisions on who to hire, promote, develop, etc. An HR function that takes ownership of strategic people outcomes is no longer merely facilitating people decisions but instead driving them and having a profound impact on the organisation. This also allows the HR department to attach a dollar value to the work they are doing.

This would make it extremely hard for business leaders to ignore the importance of the team. HR is not a cost centre; it is a value creation centre, and HR needs to begin to articulate this. An easy example to explain this would be employee attrition. Research consistently puts the cost of attrition for an employee at somewhere between 6–9 months of their annual salary. The reason for this is simple. When an employee resigns, they naturally begin to slow down. They are not as productive as an employee working at their full potential. It is also incredibly rare for an organisation to have a replacement lined up with sufficient time for a handover before the employee leaves. This means that a lot of knowledge is lost in transition and the role itself is often completely unproductive for at least a few weeks until the new person starts. Then, when the new person starts, it will take them time to get up to speed before they are truly effective. On top of this 6–9 months cost of attrition to the employee is the hidden costs that are often overlooked. An example would be the rest of the team becoming less productive because they will need to perform certain activities to cover for the fact that the team is now short of at least one person.

In addition, the manager is going to also have to step in and help out, taking time away from other duties they are required to perform. They will also need to spend time reviewing CVs, speaking to recruiters, interviewing candidates, etc. Furthermore, there is also the cost of recruiting. The team need to post job advertisements, talent acquisition team members are required to spend time on helping with replacing the new hire, and there may be recruitment agency fees, etc. Plus, the higher the attrition rate, the more members of talent acquisition and the more job post licenses that are required, and so on. So, when all is said and done, research shows that the true cost of employee attrition for a mid-level employee is not 6–9 months of their salary but instead closer to 150% of their salary. The cost can be as high as 300–400% of their annual salary for a senior leader or a specific skilled expert. So, if HR can demonstrate they can reduce attrition, reduce new hire failure, increase engagement, and so on, they can also show the financial impact of this. What is even more surprising to many in HR is that they do not realise that a simple Google search will take them to several free-to-use online calculators that can show them how to calculate these figures pretty quickly. The information is widely available.

Armed with this new approach and the ability to show the impact of the work the HR team do, this provides the HR team with something they have long craved—buy-in and support from business leadership and a seat at the table. By showing that the team are no longer passengers there to merely facilitate the process but instead drive outcomes and demonstrate the value of those outcomes in financial terms, business leaders are much more willing to devote time and energy to HR programmes. I have experienced first-hand the 180-degree turn an executive leadership team will go through once they realise prioritising employee experience and engagement is worth millions of dollars to the bottom line. A large multinational company reducing attrition by just 2% is literally worth tens of millions of dollars to that organisation's bottom line. This is why organisations that win employer of choice awards outperform the share price of those who do not by almost 200%. This is also why I state in the very first paragraph of this book that businesses with higher levels of employee engagement make two and a half times more money than other businesses.

Employee experience and engagement are not a nice to have; it is a business necessity. By linking people outcomes to financial performance, business leaders will understand that every employee touchpoint becomes a key battleground for success. Basics, like ensuring managers are well trained and suitable for the position before becoming managers, will be a key starting point. But even small items, like having an employee's favourite 3 pm snack delivered to them on their first day, will be important. After all, an employee-centric organisation is going to find it easier to attract and keep people, and this will show in better financial results as a happy workforce is a productive workforce. But the only way to get to this point is to shift from a traditional HR team focused on facilitating the process to one that drives and owns key strategic items. It would be great for business leaders to start by empowering the HR team, but the change has to come from HR themselves. If a business leader has never seen the value of an HR team, it is because the HR team have never demonstrated their value. So, it all begins with the HR team

18

proactively taking ownership and driving change within both themselves and the organisation as a whole.

Agile HR

The concept of Agile is becoming more and more prevalent within business. In fact, it is rare these days to speak to a business leadership team without them articulating their desire for their organisation to either adopt Agile in its entirety or at least shift towards being a more Agile organisation. This is for a good reason, as Agile principles are foundational to delivering exceptional levels of performance and innovation. However, despite most organisations wanting to move in this direction, the majority are failing to realise their ambitions. This is because they are running into two typical showstoppers. The first is that most of these organisations fundamentally misunderstand what Agile is. The second is that organisations attempt to implement Agile within the business but often overlook the HR department. Yet, if Agile is to take hold within an organisation, then the HR team must first be aligned to Agile ways of working.

Let's start with how and why organisations misunderstand what Agile is. Many make the mistake of thinking that Agile is a specific methodology or process. It isn't. Agile, at its core, is a philosophy. Agile can be defined as the ability to create and respond to change. It is a way to allow individuals and businesses to deal with and ultimately succeed in an uncertain and turbulent environment. Or, to put it more simply and to quote the legendary boxer Mike Tyson: 'Everyone has a plan until they get punched in the mouth'. Agile is about being able to deal with and respond

19

to getting punched in the mouth and to ensure you don't just survive but thrive. This is why the authors of *The Agile Manifesto* chose to use the word 'Agile' as the label for the whole philosophy. It is a word that perfectly represents the need to effectively adapt and respond to circumstances that is at the core of successful change management. If you get punched in the mouth, it is probably a good idea to do something different rather than just plough on ahead, doing things how they have always been done or sticking to the pre-defined plan you had set out in advance. So, Agile is really about helping you understand what is going on in the environment you are in today, identifying the uncertainty you are facing, and figuring out how to adapt as you go along.

This also means that the Agile approach doesn't end. You might stop yourself from getting punched in the face, but then someone throws a punch at your rib cage. So, you constantly adjust your game plan and avoid getting fixated on one particular approach or strategy. This is probably summed up best by *The Agile Manifesto*. The Manifesto champions the idea of individuals and interactions over process and tools. It promotes the concept of responding to change over following a plan. It explains the need to focus on working on the problem as opposed to focusing on documentation. The manifesto also encourages the concept of collaborating with the relevant impacted parties (customers, end users, etc.) over simply looking at contract negotiations. Unfortunately, many organisations continue to put far too much emphasis on the need to have the right process, policies, tools, and documentation rather than pragmatically pivoting as required. And this is exactly why they struggle to reap the benefits of Agile.

This shift to an Agile mindset enables a pragmatic focus on adding value to customers, businesses, employees, and so on without needing to have a perfect solution up front. Many in HR often speak about the need for HR to add more value without quite knowing how they can do this. The answer within Agile is really quite simple: focus on what the key pain points are (the punches in the mouth) and then adjust the approach accordingly. The new solution doesn't have to be perfect, but it should be a step in the right direction, and then this approach can be further refined via constant iteration. This is why Agile is consistently more effective than the traditional 'Waterfall' approach that businesses typically use.

To explain further, let's assume the organisation uses an employee onboarding form. Within an Agile environment, the form might be updated dozens of times throughout the year as new information comes to light. A new box might be added, and some fields might be taken away as they aren't really that relevant. It is a constant, ongoing, iterative, and pragmatic approach to the shifting needs of the organisation, and decisions can be taken by those on the ground to update accordingly without needing to run every change up the chain of command. Conversely, a waterfall approach would involve gathering all of the feedback at the end of the year, implementing some agreed changes with the approval of leadership, and then everyone is forced to stick to that format for the rest of the year as that is the form that has been approved to use. If people want changes, they can make suggestions, but the team will only look at it next year when the next version will be released. The Agile approach allows the team to respond much more effectively throughout the year to meet the changing needs and expectations of the organisation.

This approach of incremental or iterative change also has a secondary effect of making it more likely that change will succeed. One of the key reasons why change fails to take hold within an organisation is because human beings are ultimately creatures of habit. In fact, there is research that shows that most of what we do is nothing more than a set of habits and breaking these habits is incredibly difficult. So, simply because an organisation has decided something will now be done differently doesn't mean that it will be done differently. This is a large part of why digital transformations in many organisations fail. The organisation may have rolled out a fancy new system, but there is often very little focus on changing the behaviours of the team. Therefore, just expecting the team to do something in a completely different way on Monday because someone shared a couple of slides or showed someone a new system just isn't going to happen. This is why many big systems or process rollouts fail. The new system or process is great, but when organisations look into adoption, the take-up is incredibly slow, and it can take 18 months or even longer for the new ways of working to take hold. So, rather than expecting people to go from 10% to 100% in one go, Agile allows for natural evolution to take place. By taking smaller steps along the way to go from, say, 10% to 20% is a lot easier and can be done a lot quicker with much less disruption. You then take the lessons from that and use that to go to 25% or

33%, and so on. This makes the changes made more likely to take hold and be sustainable.

So, we have covered how organisations often misinterpret what Agile is along with what it actually is. The other common showstopper to Agile becoming the norm within an organisation is due to overlooking the HR department. This is because if a team is operating in a truly Agile way, the ways of working break pretty much all of the traditional HR processes and structures. For example, it is quite common for organisations to have a fairly well-established organisation structure. The organisation will be broken down into departments with leaders, managers, team leaders, individual contributors, and so on. However, within Agile, it is quite common for people to be working across the organisation because they are no longer attached to performing a set of specific tasks. Instead, they are aligned to solving a set of specific challenges which means they will need to work with multiple parties. This means that their manager within the organisational structure will have very little oversight in what they are doing every day.

A software developer would spend most of their time working directly with the relevant business team as opposed to getting instructions from their software development manager. This is how the concept of Agile 'Squads' works. As such, how do you structure the organisation? Do you have each of the relevant software developers report into the relevant business units? How would the business units know how to hire or assess a software developer's work when they have no technical knowledge? Who would set the goals and objectives for the person? Who would do the performance reviews? How do you set goals and objectives when the person is solving different problems every month, and often the problems may not even be known in advance? It is obviously not impossible to solve these problems, but it does require HR to operate in a different way. Otherwise, what often happens is that teams simply refuse to collaborate. Why would the manager allow their staff to spend 80% of their time working on projects for other teams when their entire bonus and performance review is on their own work being delivered? There is no incentive to do so. Likewise, why would an employee want to go and spend their time working on a load of extra projects that aren't part of their performance goals within their own department and therefore won't impact their performance review? So, in order to enable Agile ways of working within an organisation, HR must be involved in supporting the transition to Agile. If the business does not include HR and/or HR failing to amend its own ways of working to accommodate Agile ways of working always leads to a failed attempt to embrace Agile. The silos created by org structures, performance management processes, and so on will disincentivise staff and management from embracing it.

If HR teams want to deliver disproportionate value, then in addition to enabling an Agile environment, HR should also remove their own silos. Rather than having multiple teams or departments within HR, such as talent management, learning and development, talent acquisition, reward, operations, and HR business partners, the team should be shaped around outcomes. How this would typically work is that you would set up teams or 'squads' based on each person's capability and the problems that need to be solved. This would help HR to solve various problems they have long struggled with. Let us take an easy example of employee attrition. Who is responsible for combatting attrition? The Talent Acquisition team is responsible for hiring talent, and if they are consistently leaving, does that mean the talent is either not good enough, or they aren't a fit for the company? There is the learning and development team which are meant to be training and upskilling employees and helping them to grow, which should make them want to stay with the organisation. The talent management team should be looking at things such as succession planning and career development, so if people are leaving for better opportunities, should talent management be doing more? On the other hand, the HR Business Partner is supposed to be working with the managers to solve employee issues in advance so that attrition doesn't happen. Then we have the rewards team, which are supposed to be designing attractive salary and benefits packages for the employees, so why are they going elsewhere for a better offer?

The answer, of course, is that all of these teams, plus the hiring managers are responsible for employee attrition. But one of the reasons why most HR teams and organisations fail to combat the issue of attrition is because there is no joined-up approach. Each team is doing their own part in isolation, often failing to communicate with the other teams and, therefore, this disjointed approach fails to provide any tangible outcomes. However, if you organise members of the HR team around outcomes, you will then end up with a member of each HR team as part of an employee attrition squad along with the relevant managers who were experiencing attrition. They would then be able to create an end-to-end approach that would ensure all bases are covered. The team can then be judged on the outcome, i.e., did the solutions they came up with reduce attrition and even attach a dollar value to the outcome? But the only way to do this is to break the silos.

This means you do not have a rewards team or a talent management team, etc. Instead, you have 'pools of capability' that you are able to deploy against relevant challenges. This means you would have a group of people who are experts at assessing and selecting talent, which would be your TA team. Another group of people that are able to design incentives and link them to performance outcomes would be the people who make up your reward team. A further pool of capability that is able to develop solutions to solve knowledge gaps in your learning and development team and so on across the rest of the team. You then attach individuals from the relevant pools of capability to tackle various outcomes. One outcome, as we have discussed, would be employee attrition. Another outcome that could be tackled could be improving management capability within the organisation. There could be another around creating or embedding organisational values and culture and so on and so forth across key outcomes and challenges. This Agile approach will allow for a much more impactful solution than simply asking one team to try and tackle something for which they don't have control of 80% of the variables in a silo.

Applying Design Thinking

In addition to aligning the team to focus on outcomes as opposed to siloed sets of activities, there is one other thing the team will need to do—design solutions to those problems. This may seem simple enough, but if that were true, then most organisations would have solved these problems a long time ago. The truth is that in both HR and the wider business, there is a long history of teams treating the symptoms and not the cause. This is why problems persist year after year despite organisations thinking they are taking action to combat those challenges. It is also why research consistently shows there is a disconnect between business leaders and people on the ground, whether they are employees or customers. Business leaders consistently think they are doing something to address concerns, and the customers or employees completely disagree. An example of this which I share in *The Talent Acquisition Handbook: A Practical Guide to Candidate Experience*, relates to research from PWC that was published by Forbes. The research found that 87% of business leaders think consumers trust their organisation and the same research found that only 30% of their consumers actually say they trust their organisation. Similar research consistently finds a disconnect between leaders and employees.

A classic example of organisations treating the symptoms and not the cause is with employee engagement. It is quite common for organisations to opt for some sort of superficial fix. The fix is usually to try and make the office more fun, so they will throw some sort of party or put a pool table in the office or something along those lines. This allows management to say they are doing something, but in reality, your employees were not disengaged because there was not a pool table in the office or not more after-work drinks. Likewise, paying people more doesn't work because people are still going to leave regardless of pay if the environment is bad. This is because after the party, game of pool, or receiving the latest paycheque, they are still going to have to deal with a toxic boss that makes their life hell on a daily basis. They may still face discrimination or whatever other reasons it is they are highlighting. Therefore, regardless of the actions management think they have taken to solve the problem, staff don't feel anything has been done because a pizza party doesn't stop them from being treated like crap by their boss every day.

This is why design thinking is becoming more and more important to organisations. Design Thinking is essentially an approach that allows teams to diagnose the root cause of problems and come up with creative solutions to solve them. It has been popularised by various Silicon Valley businesses to enable a great customer experience, but the truth is that anyone can use the approach to solve anything. The key to its success is in understanding that experience will always be defined by how the person going through the experience feels about their experience. You don't get to tell your customers how they should feel when using your product and, likewise, you don't get to tell your employees how they should feel about their treatment. Design Thinking methodology, therefore, lays out a 5-step approach to ensuring a business understands how its users (whether customers, employees, candidates, or any other group) feel, to define why that is, and to design solutions to improve it. Within an HR and employee experience context, this means that when using design thinking, an HR team will be able to identify and solve the real problem at the heart of an HR metric. The 5 steps within design thinking are often referred to as empathise, define, ideate, prototype, and test. So, let's look at how each of these phases can help improve employee experience.

Empathise

The first phase within design thinking is a lot easier said than done. It is to take off the rose-tinted glasses as to your own personal views on what may be the problem—and begin to look at things from the employee's perspective. You don't get to tell employees how to feel about certain things; instead, you have to start by understanding how they feel about certain things and why that is. Without doing this properly, you will always treat the symptoms and not the cause. For example, research shows that there is a less than 1% chance of employees becoming disengaged after receiving negative feedback if they feel their strengths are valued. Yet only 14% of employees feel the yearend review motivates them to do well. Why? Because employees often feel the yearend review is focused on all of the things they haven't done well, and there is no recognition for what they have done well. Likewise, because they have not received any feedback throughout the year, most employees expect they have done a good job because they have no evidence to the contrary. In addition, research shows that employees are more likely to become disengaged if they do not receive feedback instead of receiving negative feedback. So, all of this, along with various other factors, will contribute to a sense of disengagement among staff. All of these issues and more may be present in some teams, and others may only have one or two of the elements. But I can almost guarantee that there is not a group of employees that is upset there is not a pool table in the office or a pizza party after work on a Wednesday.

So, in order to solve the employee experience challenges within your organisation, you must listen to what your people are telling you. If the HR or Business Leadership team do not seek feedback, then they are never going to be able to combat the challenges. You might not like what your people are telling you, but you have to be willing to listen and understand; otherwise, you are always going to have the same problems again and again as you are not solving them. Feedback can be derived from various channels. The employee engagement results are always a good starting point. But there should also be feedback from stay and exit interviews. Feedback from websites such as Glassdoor, feedback gathered from one-to-one meetings, formal and informal observations, and workshops designed to understand how staff truly feel about certain things. All of this data should then be put together to create an accurate understanding of how your people truly feel, regardless of whether or not that view is popular.

Define

Once the work has been done to understand exactly how employees are feeling in a certain scenario, the next step is to further work with them to define exactly why that is. For example, you may understand that employees are generally unhappy with their managers at yearend review, but why specifically are they? What is it that managers are doing? The aim is to define the specific question and problem statement the team need to address. When this is done correctly, it can result in some truly eye-opening insights for those involved. This is because the answer is often rarely found in the most obvious of places. An example of this that I always like to share relates to a client who wanted help to improve their employee referral programmes. They had tried all of the usual tricks, such as

30

offering higher referral bonuses and revamping the referral process, yet their employees were still not referring people to the organisation. The one thing they had not done was to actually look at the engagement results of the organisation or speak to members of staff about why they were not referring people. A quick glance at the employee engagement results revealed the employees were incredibly disengaged. To this day, it is one of the lowest engagement scores I have ever seen for an organisation. A series of sharing sessions were held across the organisation, and it became very clear what problem needed to be addressed. The problem was not that they were not referring people to the organisation; the problem was that none of them thought the working environment was great. So, none of them wanted to recommend it as a place to work to their friends and peers.

By taking the time to define the true problem statement using a design thinking approach of putting the employees at the centre of understanding what's happening and why, it allows for the true root cause to be identified. This means the problem statement under design thinking would be something like 'How do we create a company culture that makes our employees feel proud to work here?' Whereas the more traditional approach to problem-solving both in HR and elsewhere would focus on a symptom of the problem, such as 'How do we get our employees to refer more people?' This is what I mean by establishing the root cause. Something such as employees being unhappy about the working environment can manifest in multiple ways. Employees might refrain from recommending the company as a place to work. Alternatively, a disengaged workforce is more likely to see an

31

increase in absenteeism and sick days. Perhaps attrition is a constant problem because the environment isn't great. But the truth is that all of these are symptoms of the underlying cause, which is that the employees feel the workplace is a bad environment. Therefore, efforts should be focused on the root cause of working with management to improve the working culture. It is a small nuance in language but a big difference in the overall work being done. One type of action would be focused on a task such as ensuring more employees turned up for work or referred more friends to open positions. The other type of work involves a significant revaluation of the type of environment the organisation wants to create and a re-aligning of how management conduct themselves and make decisions to help foster a better culture for employees. By doing this, more staff will want to come to work. They will want to recommend their friends, and fewer people will be consistently quitting.

Ideate

The third stage of design thinking is focused on coming up with ideas to address the root cause issues identified in the empathise and define stages of the design thinking process. At this stage, there is no bad idea. In fact, the more ideas you can generate, the better. Ideas can range from simple and basic ideas all the way to insane ideas that are so far out of the box that the box cannot even be seen anymore. But there are two things to have in place to ensure ideation increases the chances of a successful outcome. The first is to ensure all key stakeholders are part of the ideation process. Now, contrary to popular belief within the corporate world, this does not mean the most senior people within the organisation. It means those who are most directly affected. So, if you are going to come up with programmes to help create a better culture for employees, there is very little point in having your senior leadership team come up with ideas on their own. It would be much more valuable to have employees be able to directly contribute ideas. After all, they are the ones who are most directly impacted by the culture, so asking them what they would like is probably a good idea!

The second is to ensure ideation is done with a blank slate in mind. It is very common for people to limit their ideas on what they feel could be possible. For example, if a process was rubbish and causing a team lots of pain, rather than calling to have the whole process re-designed, it is very common to have the team only suggest small incremental changes. This is because they don't feel leadership would support a full re-design. Therefore, instead of creating a solution that would completely solve the problem (a new process), the team end up only making the situation slightly better. To increase the chances of successfully solving the problem, all options must be on the table during ideation—no matter how feasible they may seem at the time. Maybe replacing the entire management team is the only way to improve the culture if all of the CEOs' direct reports refuse to acknowledge there are any problems with the culture despite all of the evidence proving otherwise.

Prototype

The fourth step of design thinking revolves around creating potential solutions that can then be tested. A common mistake at this stage of problem-solving is to assume that you need to pick one idea you are going to pursue. That is not the case. There is no reason why you can't create 3, 5, or even 10 or more potential solutions to test. For example, if you are working for a large multinational company spanning multiple countries, you could design multiple solutions and try a different one in each country to see what works best. After all, the true test of problem-solving is whether or not the solution actually solved the problem. It, therefore, makes perfect sense to prototype a few different ideas to ensure the best solution is implemented at scale. This can also be incredibly useful in corporate environments where there is a lack of alignment. You don't need to decide on what to do until you have seen the results. Therefore, build out several solutions to test and learn.

Test

Finally, once the prototype solutions are ready, they should be tested in small-scale pilots to assess their effectiveness. So, if we revert back to our example of trying to improve company culture, this could mean that several ideas are tested in different countries to see the impact. One country might roll out a management training programme to show managers how to treat their people as opposed to just focusing on results. Another country might implement a new communication strategy. A third might have a weekly after-work pizza party. Then engagement scores would be monitored over the next 3–6 months to see what the impact is. There will be lessons learned, the ideas can be further refined, and then the solution (or solutions) with the best results would be rolled out across the whole organisation to address the root cause problem statement.

The Financial Benefits of HR

Have you ever heard a senior leader say that HR is a cost centre, not a profit centre? If you have been working in the industry for a while, it is almost certain that you have. But let me tell you a secret about this statement. It is wrong. In fact, not only is it wrong, but it is one of the most idiotic and short-sighted statements you will ever hear someone in leadership make. This is because a business is only as good as the quality of its people. Without people, there is no business. This is a fact. It is also a fact that a proper strategic value add HR function improves a company's ability to hire better talent more quickly, improve the capabilities of each of its employees and ensure the talent is retained for longer. If you think hiring better talent faster, improving your existing employees' level of capability, and ensuring your people stay with the business longer costs money – then you should not be a leader within a business. A well-run HR department is a value creator, not a cost centre. The reason this is not more widely understood is because the harsh truth is that very few HR teams see their role to create value. This is why we have spent most of this chapter discussing why and how HR can make the pivot from managing processes to enabling business outcomes.

HR will argue that they often struggle to get the financial backing to invest sufficiently in the team to create a strategic function. Business leaders will argue that they aren't going to invest heavily in the HR team because they are yet to see the HR team provide any value beyond ensuring the administration is done. In most instances, both parties are right. So, how do you solve this? Well, the easy solution would be for the organisation to get new leadership that has worked somewhere where the HR team were superstars, and they will invest in and champion the importance of the HR team. But let's be honest, the chances of this happening are incredibly rare. The alternative is for HR to begin to speak the business language and start discussing initiatives related to business impact. This means the team will use their newfound Agile and Design Thinking Skills to come up with new ideas and then explain the financial impact these ideas will have if they work.

Now, believe it or not, this is actually really easy to do. One of the easiest ways to do this is to discuss the cost of hiring. Research from McKinsey shows that 82% of CEOs feel their company is unable to attract the right talent. This naturally impacts business results and is why organisations are incredibly keen to improve their hiring strategies. They are also very aware that the cost of hiring is substantial. Organisations spend over $500 billion a year on recruitment fees to third-party recruiters. Therefore, if your talent acquisition team is able to implement a great new sourcing strategy such as the ones outlined in my book *The Talent Acquisition Handbook*. then you are going to be able to show a substantial saving on third-party spending. This can be done by hiring more through referrals, training more talent so that more vacancies are filled by internal resources and replacing them with more junior ones, or having the talent acquisition team directly hire more people, among other things. If the strategy is a success, then you are able to show the value of the talent acquisition team and thus get more investment to improve things even further.

However, the key to unlocking the true value creation of the HR department is to attach a financial value to the productivity of employees. This enables the HR team to show the financial benefit of a wide-ranging set of HR programmes. The productivity of your employees naturally has a huge impact on the performance of the company. In addition, most of the things that impact productivity link directly to people-related programmes. This is because employee engagement and employee productivity are interlinked. It is why I outline in the very first paragraph of this book that businesses with higher levels of engagement make two and half times more money than businesses that don't.

So, how do you calculate productivity? There is a simple formula that you can use. One of the easiest ways to start out is to simply divide total output by total input. This would mean dividing the total revenue the organisation made by the number of hours employees worked. If your organisation made $800,000 in revenue and the total hours worked by employees was 15,000, then you would divide 800,000 by 15,000. This means that an hour of work results in $53 of output. You could then use this to determine how much productivity is generated per employee in a day, week, month, quarter, etc. This will provide the HR team with a baseline to use and can and should also be linked to the engagement results of the organisation. Then, the success or failure of HR programmes can be linked directly to both engagement scores and the productivity of the workforce.

For example, let us assume the engagement results show that employees consistently complain that the organisation does not invest in their development. The HR team could then design and roll out a new employee development programme and link its success or failure to next year's engagement and productivity figures. So, if 60% of employees complained they were not provided with development opportunities, and then in the following year's results only 35% of employees made the same complaint, it is clear the programme is having an effect. This should also likely lead to a reduction in attrition as fewer employees are going to feel they need to leave in order to progress further in their careers. Furthermore, if employees are being upskilled and developed, they are also going to have a higher level of capability than before. So, all of this should lead to not only higher levels of engagement but also higher levels of productivity. Therefore, the HR team would not only champion the traditional HR metrics but also show that instead of $53 of productivity per hour, the organisation is now generating $68 per hour.

This same approach can be used across numerous other HR-related programmes. For example, if an organisation was able to improve its hiring process to reduce the hiring time by two weeks, that means new hires are being onboarded two weeks earlier. Thus, the organisation is now getting an extra two weeks of productivity from all new hires. This is all before adding on the major financial impacts of reducing attrition as well. It is widely proven by research, including the US Government's own department of Labour, that the cost of hiring is typically one-third of the new hire's salary. The cost is not just as simple as paying a recruitment agency fee. It will include things such as having to do employment checks, job adverts, lost productivity of the manager and team members who have to take time out from doing their job to interview, and potential sign-on bonuses or pay increases to bring someone new on. So, if you have 100 people in your business and the average salary is $45,000, and you must replace 15 employees a year, that costs you $225,000. And that is before we even consider the cost of onboarding or training, and we have not even begun to talk about the cost of lost productivity. If you are a large multinational corporation with 10,000 employees, these same figures mean that the cost of hiring is $22.5 million.

In addition to the specific costs related to hiring, there are also wider productivity costs caused by employee turnover. Research has shown that the productivity lost because of employee turnover is of significant value. A conservative cost estimate would be 50% of the employee's salary; most research puts the figure closer to 75% of the annual salary. This figure factors in the average time from when an employee quits or resigns, the vacancy being open with no one doing the job, and then even when a new hire starts, the time it takes for them to get fully up to speed. So, if we return to our example above and use the conservative 50% figure, the same small business of 100 employees is not only having to pay $225,000 to hire 15 replacement employees, but they are also losing an additional $337,500 in productivity because of employee turnover. That means the total cost of employee turnover for them is $562,500. The large multinational with 10,000 employees is losing an additional $33,750,000 in productivity plus the hiring cost of

$22.5 million, which means their total cost of turnover is $56,250,000.

I am, of course, keeping these examples high level based on an average salary, and you would, of course, be able to use your own internal productivity figures to come up with a more accurate figure of what 33% or 50% would equate to within your own organisation. But keeping in mind those figures, imagine what the financial benefit for the organisation is by creating an HR programme to reduce attrition from 15% to 10%. That small business of 100 employees saves the company $75,000 a year by not having to absorb the cost of as many hires. The company would also ensure the workforce is more productive and an extra $112,500 is gained in productivity. This means a strategic HR team just in these two areas would save the organisation $187,500. For that multinational corporation with 10,000 employees, that is a saving of $7.5 million just on hiring costs plus an additional $11,250,000 in productivity, resulting in a saving of over $18 million. And all of this is before factoring in the additional productivity benefits the team would likely enable through its programmes, such as improving capability, and so on.

It is incredibly rare for any competent business leader to consider such an impact by a department as a cost to the organisation. More importantly, these are just some surface-level examples of the huge variety of financial benefits a strategic HR function can bring to a business's bottom line. But it is on the HR team themselves to begin to shift from managing the process to proactively designing programmes that contribute to business outcomes. On top of this, they must take the lead in beginning to calculate and advocate for the value they contribute to the organisation as a result of these programmes. Failure to do so will lead to the HR team continuing to be seen as a cost centre as opposed to a value creator.

Chapter 2: The Importance of Management Capability

A lot is written about employee engagement and experience, but there is one truth that underpins all others. If you have an employee engagement and employee experience problem (and therefore likely an attrition problem), then you have a management capability problem. You can have the best HR team in the world with the best HR policies in the world, but all of this becomes irrelevant if the managers within your organisation lack the required capability to lead people effectively. Thus, any attempt to improve employee experience and, therefore, engagement must start with management capability. Failure to do this will mean there will be a limit on how much employee experience and engagement can be improved.

This is often an uncomfortable truth for those in HR and Business Leadership positions. After all, it is often a lot easier to point fingers at employees or 'market conditions' than to speak truth to power and hold those in management responsible. But this is a necessary step that must be taken in order to deliver a great employee experience, boost engagement and deliver outstanding business results. For example, your organisation could have the best training and development programme available. But if a manager refuses to provide growth opportunities to employees or to apply the skills they learn—then they are not going to have a great employee experience and will become disengaged. Your organisation can have the best flexible working policies available, but if an employee's manager bans remote working in the team, forces the team to come in every day, and is constantly calling staff outside of working hours to have them complete certain tasks, then the employee experience is not a good one. Your reward team could design the best salary and benefits package in the industry, but if your employees are working for a tyrant of a manager who bullies their team members, then they aren't having a great employee experience. Your organisation could be a huge champion and advocate of equality, but if a manager is consistently making racist, homophobic, sexist, or other sorts of disparaging remarks, then the employee experience is not great.

Sure, you can argue that if any of these kinds of things happened in the office, or the numerous other examples of how a manager impacts staff in a negative way, then someone would step in and fix it. But the truth is that people don't step in outside of a handful of truly well-run organisations that prioritise employee experience and engagement. If it were normal for organisations to step in and intervene, then organisations who prioritise engagement and experience would not make two and a half times more money than businesses that don't. Everyone would be doing it, and there would be no competitive advantage or benefit to looking after your people. The reason there is such a benefit is because it is not common, and as I outline in my book *The Manager Handbook*, there are numerous reasons for this.

Research has shown that a person's direct manager is responsible for 70% of the variance within employee engagement. Simply improving management capability could lead to as much as a 70% increase in engagement. It is also why research consistently shows that the leading cause of employee attrition is someone's direct manager. People don't leave companies, they leave managers. This has been proven time and time again for decades. It isn't the only reason employees leave, but it is overwhelmingly the leading cause, and it isn't even close. Therefore, if you want to improve employee experience and engagement, you have to start with management capability. But this isn't about simply pointing the finger at management and blaming them. The truth is that most in management are set up for failure and provided very little support. Research has shown that 90% of managers have little or no management capability. This is because nearly every organisation promotes their people based on their ability to perform their last job well, not on their ability to perform the next job well. Sure, someone may be an amazing software developer, but this does not mean they are going to be a good leader of others. Someone's ability to write computer code has absolutely no bearing on their ability to coach, develop and lead other software developers. One day they are writing code, then the next day, they are promoted and expected to know how to interview and hire, set goals, assess performance, and build culture and engagement with practically no training or guidance.

This is often referred to as the 'Peter Principle'. Because promotions are treated as a reward, almost everyone will eventually get promoted to a level of incompetence. This is because each new promotion leads to a different set of challenges requiring different skills. A software developer writing code requires a different set of skills to a manager of a team of software developers. A manager of software developers requires a different skill set to a senior manager overseeing a technology system implementation. A senior manager overseeing a technology system implementation requires a different skill set to a director overseeing an entire technology department. Very few people are able to continue to adjust and develop the new skills required to succeed at the next level. This leads to a large number of incompetent people in roles they are unable to excel in. It also leads to a very unhappy group of employees working for those people. Forbes has previously shared research that indicates 98% of managers believe that managers within their own organisation require more training. The research further indicated that 40% of managers are unprepared for management in any capacity. And 87% of managers also wished they had been provided with more training when they first became a manager. The truth is that most managers are learning on the job and trying to figure things out for themselves.

This issue is further compounded by the fact that most organisations do not assess their managers on their ability to actually manage people. Nobody says anything if you have a sales manager who is hitting their sales targets but has consistently high attrition. If you have a software development manager who has staff consistently quitting due to the workload, but projects are still delivered, this is fine. What these organisations fail to understand is that these results would be even better if the team were managed properly. According to research from Mercer, 70% of businesses do not rate their managers based on their people leadership capabilities. In addition, only 9% of organisations link a manager's pay and bonus to their people management skills. But if an organisation wants to create an incredible employee experience, boost employee engagement, and reap the business benefits, then this needs to change.

Google is one of the best case studies in defining the impacts of investing in management capability. Ironically, they achieved this accidentally while actually setting out to prove that the manager's impact on a team was irrelevant. In 2002 they tested a hypothesis that good employees did not require management. They proposed that the quality of the manager did not matter and that they were merely an additional layer of bureaucracy. They assumed that if you hire good people, they will know what to do and don't need some middle manager overseeing what they do. They called this Project Oxygen, and it was a spectacular failure. Google discovered that most people are lost without direction and support from management. Staff were directionless and, therefore, unable to work towards a common goal without someone in authority to lead the way. So, without any managers, their people had no idea what to do. It was a disaster. As a result of this, they pivoted and spent the next several years running a series of studies and pilots to understand what key traits their top managers and leaders exhibited and if they could be trained in others. The results were profound and showed that 75% of their worst-performing managers experienced a significant increase in performance by improving their management capability. This led to the organisation embedding these principles across the organisation in 2010. Google's business results have since spoken for themselves, and the share price has risen circa 900% over the next 10+ years.

Leadership Development

Management capability is essential, as we have now established. Therefore, a cornerstone of HR programmes has to revolve around the development of its current and future people leaders. It is a foundational pillar to enabling employee experience, employee engagement, and outsized business outcomes. Unfortunately, leadership development is often an afterthought in many organisations. As we have already discussed, most in management are just expected to know how to manage people, but the truth is that they don't. One of the easiest ways to begin to improve management capability is to create a 'manager essentials programme' that runs throughout the year and is mandatory for all people managers to attend. It should cover all of the essentials and consistently reinforce what good looks like year on year. This could involve things such as setting goals at the start of the year, dealing with the inevitable attrition that arises after bonuses are paid, shaping new roles and job descriptions, assessing and selecting talent in interviews, having performance conversations, building culture and engagement, and so on and so forth. This should then set a baseline for the organisation that can be built on. This would naturally then be augmented by specific training for specific managers or leaders based on individual needs. For example, if a manager is consistently being rated low in engagement surveys for their ability to provide learning opportunities or career development to the team.

This type of essentials programme and the supplementary training can be run either by the in-house team or external partners, depending on the capability of the internal team. But it is also incredibly important to get the content right. Organisations that do provide leadership or management training spend roughly $400 billion a year on it. But despite this huge outlay, only 7% feel that it was helpful. This is usually for one of two reasons. The first is that it's so high level or theoretical that the people manager has no idea how to put it into practice. A people manager does not need to understand complex frameworks and methodologies. They need practical advice and guidance on what to do during day-to-day people management interactions. For example, if there is a deadline on Friday that is critical and cannot be missed, yet a key member of the team has a death in the family—what are they supposed to do? Are they supposed to force the employee to come in and work even though they have a death in the family because the deadline is non-negotiable, or let them have time off and likely miss the deadline?

The second reason is that the training is provided too late to have an impact. This is why nearly 40% of CEOs fail within their first 18 months. Whilst there are those who want to be better, there are also those who think they don't need training. This is usually more common in senior level leadership training. This is because teaching an old dog new tricks is extremely hard. If you have someone working for more than 20 years and has become head of their department, it is very hard for that person to accept they are not doing certain things well. After all, they will feel they have been managing people for many years. They have had success and made it to the level of department head. How could they achieve that if they were doing things wrong? But as organisations promote based on the performance in the last job and not the ability to perform the next role, they will lack the capability and need to improve. This issue is further compounded by the fact that most organisations do not assess their managers on their ability to actually manage.

Once the manager essentials programme is in place, the next step is to design a programme to reassess how your organisation promotes (or hires) people into people management roles. As previously mentioned, research has shown that up to 9 out of 10 in management don't have the required people management capabilities. This research is in line with broader research across the general population, showing that roughly 10% of the general population have natural leadership skills. An example I use in my book, *The Manager Handbook,* is as follows. Which salesperson should you choose to promote? Employee A, the clear number one salesperson, who made twice as much money as anyone else but has a reputation for being rude and disrespectful to others. Or Employee B, the number 6 salesperson who also beat their sales targets but made 3 times less than the number one salesperson, but who consistently goes out of their way to help others? Pretty much every single organisation in the world makes the mistake of choosing Employee A when it is clearly the wrong choice.

It is clear that Employee A will make a bad manager despite being a great individual salesperson, but an organisation would worry about losing a high performer if they are not promoted. However, by making Employee A the manager, they are going to end up losing most of the other salespeople. Employee A may be great as an individual, but they can't make enough sales alone to make up for losing an entire team. More importantly, as a manager, Employee A shouldn't still be performing the role as a front-line salesperson. They should be focused on getting everyone else to sell, so you are going to have a dip in their sales figures anyway. On the other hand, Employee B has not only been a success themselves, and may not have been number one, but they beat their sales targets and have demonstrated the right kind of behaviour you would want from a manager within the company to support and grow others.

So, as part of the new programme that addresses how people are promoted, an organisation should include qualifiers to ensure the employee who is going to become a manager has demonstrated they have the capabilities to lead others. This should not be based entirely on the view of the leader making the promotion decision either. This is because we know it is rare for a leadership team to prioritise a person's ability to manage others as a key criterion for promotion. Therefore, a better demonstration of capability would be to have three junior people within the organisation endorse the employee's promotion to manager by providing testimony as to how the person has helped them grow. This would allow for the organisation to foster a culture where employees know that if they want to climb the ladder, then they have to focus on coaching and developing others and not just screwing others over to make themselves look good. Likewise, perhaps part of the promotion case for the new manager focuses on them working with a charity or education institute where they have devoted a couple of hours a week to coaching and mentoring others. There are, of course, numerous other ways to ensure the person being promoted displays the right traits in advance. But remember, the aim is to ensure the person displays the capabilities required to excel in the next role and that a promotion is not merely a reward for performing the last role well.

This should conclude the second pillar of your leadership development strategy. The first is setting up a management essentials programme, and the second is to be focused on ensuring anyone new who enters the group has the required capabilities to excel. The third pillar to ensure you are adequately developing your management group should be focused on identifying who your future managers and leaders are and creating management and leadership development plans for them—well in advance of them moving into such roles. For example, someone may join you as a new graduate trainee, but it could be clear that they have natural leadership characteristics. This person should be provided with training to nurture and develop those skills as soon as they are identified. The truth is that an organisation's next group of successful leaders are unlikely to be superstars as individual contributors. This is because the characteristics required to be a great individual executor are not the same as those required to support and coach a group to perform well. In fact, organisations consistently tag their potential future leaders as disruptive employees. This is because they are seen as junior people who are there to do what they are told, yet they will question and challenge why certain things are done in a certain way. You do not want your future managers and leaders to be order takers who will do what they are told. You want your future managers and leaders to proactively improve both their team and the wider organisation.

It is, therefore, important to identify those individuals who are going to push the organisation forward. The good news is that

51

your company does not need to have a robust team of experts internally that are able to assess and identify your organisation's future leaders. Instead, the company should make use of one of the widely available psychometric assessment tools that is able to identify individuals who have a propensity towards leading as opposed to following. It would not take much effort to ensure everyone in the organisation is assessed every couple of years, and all new hires are assessed as they join the organisation. The team can then work to design a programme to ensure that these junior people with a natural inclinations towards management are prepared and primed well in advance of becoming managers. Additionally, they should be provided with assignments and opportunities to put those learnings into practice with stretch assignments and projects.

The final step to embedding programmes that enable management capability to thrive throughout the organisation is to shift to a culture where management and leadership are seen as a separate career path from technical know-how. In many organisations career paths are vertical as opposed to horizontal. Someone may start out as a trainee in finance. They eventually get promoted to an assistant accountant, then an accountant. Next is to become a financial controller, finance director, and CFO before eventually becoming CEO. Then the CEO struggles, and there is a near 40% failure of CEOs within the first 18 months. This can be no surprise. This is because the job of a CEO and leaders, in general, is to lead an organisation or a department. A good leader, for the most part, does not need to be a technical expert within a certain field.

The Chief Technology Officer is not an expert in Infrastructure, Core Applications Development, Helpdesk Support, Cyber Security, and so on. This is before you even begin to factor in all of the different systems and languages. Most people dedicate an entire career to being an expert in one part of one system. No one is an expert in every piece of technology in the entire technology department. The Chief Technology Officer's job is to ensure they have highly capable managers leading each of those teams and that the teams under them are able to execute to get the required business results. The Chief Technology Officer is not going to be personally hiring the infrastructure team, but they would be hiring the Head of Infrastructure, who needs to lead the team. The same is true of a CEO. Is the CEO an expert in sales, marketing, finance, HR, operations, and so on? Of course not. But the CEO does not have to be. They have to be able to hire people with the relevant capabilities to lead those departments and then set effective goals and provide the relevant support to ensure they are successful. Therefore, the priority focus should be on managers being able to lead and develop this so they can apply these management capabilities across multiple teams and departments. Not only will this strengthen the pool of management capability within the organisation, but it will also create a much more agile and flexible management group who understand a lot more of the organisation than just their own department or area of technical expertise.

Succession Planning

In order to effectively build a high level of management capability, it is essential to integrate rather than separate leadership development and succession planning. This is because leadership development is the most effective when an organisation takes a long-term view of developing the capability of its management group. A holistic end-to-end view of leadership development, such as the approach outlined in the leadership development section, inevitably touches on multiple succession planning topics. After all, succession planning is about ensuring there is a strong internal pipeline of talent ready to step up and take over from the current group of leaders.

A failure to integrate leadership development and succession planning throughout the end-to-end lifecycle leads to a sporadic set of initiatives that fail to deliver an adequate return on investment. For example, arranging an ad-hoc training session for an hour over lunch to address staff complaining about a lack of support from management is neither going to solve the short-term problem nor enable a strong management group to be built over the longer term. Likewise, only focusing all attention on the existing leadership group and not those lower down in the organisation pretty much ensures the same problems occur again and again. After all, when one leader leaves, you need to start by training the new person again from scratch, as they missed out on the original sessions. Therefore, the same problems will continue to permeate the organisation. In addition, the organisation is forced to continually try and upskill a small group who are likely to lack natural leadership instincts. After all, if there is no long-term joined-up strategy, then people will continue to be promoted as a reward for performing the last job well, not because they will excel in the last one. This means a huge amount of time and resources are going to be spent on individuals who, at best, may become an average people leader after a few years of training and support!

In fact, a key reason why most succession planning programmes fail is because they are only focused on the handful of top leadership positions. The reason for this is simple. If you are only looking to assess the quality of the leadership pipeline at the very end, you can't ensure sufficient quality makes it through to that stage to be successful. This is a common problem for most organisations, and it is why less than 20% of organisations report that they have a suitable internal candidate who would be able to take over from the existing CEO. This also has huge ramifications for an organisation because research has shown that homegrown CEOs (meaning CEOs promoted from within) significantly outperform CEOs hired from outside the organisation. These are not fluffy performance measures either; the research shows that outperformance occurs across seven key metrics: return on assets, equity and investment, revenue and earnings growth, earnings per share (EPS) growth, and stock-price appreciation. In fact, roughly 67% of externally hired CEOs fail to make it to their fourth anniversary with their new company. The same kind of results are seen when looking at the lower levels of the organisation too. Homegrown managers are also a lot more effective than those hired from outside the organisation.

The reason homegrown managers and leaders are more successful is quite simple. The first reason is that because they are from the existing culture, they are more likely to be a fit and understand the various internal dynamics and challenges at play. This is critical because culture fit is more important than anything else when it comes to being successful within an organisation. Someone with 70% of the technical skills that is a 100% fit for the culture will consistently outperform someone else who may be the best in the world but is unable to integrate into the culture. Unfortunately, as I outline in my book, *The Talent Acquisition Handbook: A Practical Guide to Candidate Experience,* very few organisations prioritise culture fit while hiring. This means they consistently hire people who have the skills but may not fit in. This is a key reason why research repeatedly shows that it's 50/50 as to whether or not a new hire stays with an organisation beyond 18 months. So, by growing your own managers and leaders, you overcome this significant first barrier to success. In addition, because they are homegrown, they already know which people and teams do what in the organisation, which cuts down the amount of time it takes them to be able to effect real change and impact results. Moving into management from the working level, they understand the actual pain points of those on the ground and so are able to implement more meaningful changes than a manager or leader who comes in from the outside.

The second reason why homegrown managers and leaders are more successful is that assuming the organisation is actually investing in developing and preparing its people properly for the transition into management, the organisation can better control the quality, behaviour, and values of those in charge, which increases the likelihood of them being successful. One of the key reasons why most management and leadership training fails is because it is often given too late to have an impact. As the saying goes, it is hard to teach an old dog new tricks. This is often why CEO succession planning fails. If you have someone working for more than 20 years and has become head of their department, it is very hard for that person to accept they are not doing certain things well. After all, they will feel they have been managing people for many years. They have had success and made it to the level of department head. How could they achieve that if they were doing things wrong? But as organisations promote based on the performance in the last job and not the ability to perform the next role, they will lack the capability and need to improve.

This issue is further compounded by the fact that most organisations do not assess their managers on their ability to actually manage. Therefore, aligning succession planning with leadership development and applying it not just to those at the very top of the pyramid, but all the way through the organisation, right down to the most junior, allows a company to better control the quality of the management pipeline. This allows homegrown managers to be a lot more effective. In addition, we know that 70% of businesses do not rate their managers based on their people leadership capabilities, and 9% of organisations link a manager's pay and bonus to their people management skills. This means that the likelihood of the manager you are hiring from outside being a good manager is very low. In fact, it is often the case that when it comes to people management, you are likely to need to first untrain an experienced manager and then train them in how to manage aligned to your own organisation's values and behaviours. It takes a lot longer and is much more difficult than simply training your own managers from scratch when they are a blank slate.

This is why succession planning (and leadership development) should be applied to the whole organisation and not just the handful of leadership roles at the top. After all, if you are not moulding your management group from the very beginning, then what is the point in moulding them at all? If an organisation can control from the very beginning all the employees that go from rank and file into supervisory positions, into middle management, then senior management, and finally leadership, the quality of the leadership pipeline within the organisation is going to be incredibly strong. It would be able to survive natural attrition and black swan events, ensuring an organisation thrives regardless of the circumstances. Therefore, it is vital that not only is training and succession planning integrated throughout the organisation, but that programmes are set up to manage the pipeline. This allows the organisations to ensure that promotions are not handed out as rewards for those who performed well in the last job but haven't displayed the characteristics to succeed in the next job. So rather than promoting that great individual contributor who consistently shows disrespectful behaviour to team members, an org would promote the good performer who takes time out of their day to coach and help other team members without being asked.

Finally, all of this should be combined with ensuring that your future managers and leaders are well rounded and have a full view of the whole organisation. It's important to remember that growth does not have to be upwards and, in fact, some of the best succession planning programs involve sideways moves. If you have a high potential leader who is a technical expert in software, they can go all the way up the ladder to become chief technology officer in theory. But do you know what would make them a better CTO when the time comes? Having a broader skill set and understanding of the business. Taking that superstar technical person and having them spend 18 months working in the marketing or sales team would do significantly more for them than promoting them to manage more software people. A CTO that understands buying habits of customers, the challenges of the salespeople selling it, and how the company markets it, would be much more valuable to the organisation. So, ensure the succession planning programme thinks of the organisation as a whole, as opposed to individual departments in silos.

Diversity in Leadership

Why is diversity important? I have sat on inclusion and diversity councils at various points in my career and also run hundreds of workshops on inclusion and diversity. And let me tell you a secret: no one has ever given me the right answer to this question when I have asked it in a business setting. I get lots of people trying to explain how it is the right thing to do, why equality is important, and so on. These are good answers, but they are not the right answer. These are what are seen in the real business world as a nice to have, but they are rarely seen as a business essential. The right answer within a business setting is that businesses with diverse leadership teams make roughly 33%

more money than businesses that do not. Don't get me wrong, all of the other reasons are important; I would not have been a champion of inclusion and diversity for all of these years if they weren't. But they are not going to convince a leadership team to change course and give it the prioritisation it deserves just because it's the right thing to do. Just as with employee experience and many other topics that are essential, but wrongly tagged as 'fluffy', the best argument is the financial argument. It is amazing how many follow-up questions you get from a C-suite when you explain they could make 33% more money by embracing diversity (and, as we have discussed, two and a half times more money than their competitors by prioritising employee experience as well).

So, let's be clear, just like employee experience is a business essential because it will allow the company to make more money, so too is diversity and inclusion a business essential. It will also allow your organisation to make a lot more money. How? It is simple. The fundamental reason is because the more people you have with a variety of different personalities and backgrounds, the more viewpoints you will have and, therefore, the better ideas you will come up with. Let me elaborate a little. The world's most popular personality assessment is the Myers-Briggs assessment, which identifies 16 different personality types. I am not aiming to get into a debate on the validity or shortcomings of the Myers-Briggs assessment but to provide a proof point that there are different personalities. Whether it is Myers-Briggs or simply your own assessment based on your own life experience, you should agree that people have different personalities. Which organisation do you think would be more successful? An organisation made up of only one type of personality where everyone thinks and acts the same way, or an organisation that has all 16 different personalities?

This fundamental choice is at the core of the inclusion and diversity debate that goes on within large corporate work environments. Ultimately, if everyone thinks and acts the same way, you will be unable to compete with another team or business that can think and act in 16 different ways. Combining all of the strengths and weaknesses of all 16 personalities will lead to better results. This is why businesses with more diversity make more money than others. The easiest way for your business to outperform is to be able to harness multiple ways of working and solutions. The best way to do that is to ensure you have a whole range of different kinds of people from different backgrounds and perspectives—all contributing to the same purpose. As a whole, the ideas and solutions they come up with will be a lot stronger than those who can only draw on one way of doing things. Remember, the 16 different personality types are also just a baseline before adding demographics on top. When you also add on the impact of race, education, age, socio-economic status, and a whole host of other criteria in how people see the world, that is an incredible competitive advantage. This is also why individuals who work internationally make up roughly 33% of high performers despite only being 1% of the global workforce. By working internationally, they see multiple ways to do the same thing and are able to therefore create something new, combining the best of what works around the world.

So, why is there not more diversity among leaders? Whether we are talking about the number of women in leadership or other minority groups, the fact is that there is a significant lack of diversity. Bias obviously plays a role, but honestly, it plays less of a role than it used to. The truth is that most organisations have invested a lot in their inclusion and diversity programmes over the past couple of decades. Don't get me wrong, as an ethnic minority myself, I am not going to sit here and claim bias doesn't exist anymore. It does. But there is a lot of will within most organisations to make more progress than they have. The uncomfortable discussion a lot of organisations seem to want to avoid having is related to the internal programmes they have set up. Ironically, a lot of the programmes that have been set up to help accelerate the promotion of women and minorities up the ladder have had the reverse effect and actually set them up for failure.

A key reason this has happened is because many organisations have taken a check-the-box approach to inclusion and diversity. So, rather than understand and fix the root cause of the issue, they have simply treated the symptoms. The way in which this often manifests is with an organisation trying to enforce arbitrary quotas to get a certain number of a demographic through to the right levels. If there are not enough women or minorities at a certain level, simply enforcing a rule that a certain percentage of people from that demographic must be in management is doomed to fail. It, more often than not, sets someone up for failure rather than success. For example, if a company arbitrarily says 40% of its leaders must be female, as many firms have chosen to do, this results in two common problems. The first of these is that any woman hired into a leadership role is often seen as being a token gesture. This cuts the authority out from beneath them before they even start, especially among those in the organisation who may hold discriminatory beliefs. The mindset of the old-fashioned misogynists internally is going to be, 'oh, she only got the job because she was a woman'. This belief will permeate even if the person put into the role is clearly the best person for the job.

This results in her not being taken seriously by some and also makes it likely that some high potential male talent internally is going to resign. They will be leaving the team simply because they feel their career path is limited due to the quota. Those individuals may not be demonstrating bias; they may likely be huge advocates of equality, but if a company is telling its male employees that even if they are great, a job must go to a woman to tick a box, why would they stick around? There is no reason for any driven professional to stick around long term if an organisation states they can't be promoted because they are from the wrong demographic. This further impacts the new female leader's performance as they end up losing one or several key performers. Therefore, the team are now less likely to succeed. Thus, the decision to promote or hire the woman into the leadership role based on a quote leaves her with no authority over the team and without several key members of staff.

The second big problem that quotas cause is that a company sometimes ends up hiring someone into a role they are not yet ready for or capable of performing—simply because they need to meet an arbitrary quota. This issue is usually made worse by the fact that the company makes a big deal out of hiring a female leader because they are box-ticking and keen to show they are on track to meet their inclusion and diversity quotas. Then what happens? Because they hired someone on a token basis who may not yet have been ready, the female leader becomes a very public failure, allowing an organisation to double down on the old misogynistic view that women can't lead. Both of these problems also play out with minority quotas as well, with minority women having it twice as bad.

In order to get more female and ethnic minority talent through to leadership levels, it is vital to shift away from these quotas. Instead, the starting point for any organisation should be to focus on the quality of its talent regardless of demographics. Quite simply, the best talent is the best talent. If that happens to be 90% male in your organisation at this very second, then that is fine. If it happens to be 90% female at this moment, that is also fine. But no good can come from arbitrarily mandating that a specific demographic must make up a certain percentage of roles. Rather than using quotas, the organisation should instead implement benchmarks to monitor whether or not their workforce is representative of the communities they are part of. This allows the organisation to avoid enforcing strict quotas that set people up for failure and instead flag areas where teams are clearly outside of norms.

For example, according to research, about 22% of software developers are women. It is a well-documented male-dominated field. We can argue about all of the ways to get more women into STEM-related careers, but that is a whole book on its own. Instead, what an organisation should do is acknowledge that the current state of the industry is as such. Therefore, assuming there is no discrimination within the organisations, women should make up about 20% of the software development team. That means 1 in 5 should be coding, the same managing, and so on. This isn't a strict quota; it's just a simple averaging exercise that if, on average, 1 in 5 software developers are women, then on average, you are going to end up hiring women for 1 in 5 vacancies. So, if your team consists of 18% or 27% women, that seems reasonable. After all, that's a fair deviation from the average, considering things such as available talent at the time, and so on. The numbers should fluctuate; there shouldn't be exactly 22%, but it should be there or thereabouts.

However, if your software development team only consists of 10% women in both team and management positions, then there is clearly an issue. That is half of the industry average. This should then be a flag as the team are way outside of industry norms, which means there must be some reason why. This would then lead to an investigation using those Agile and Design Thinking skills we discussed in Chapter 1, leading to identifying root causes and solutions to them. Perhaps there is outright discrimination within the team. Perhaps the organisations lack the required employee benefits or working environment to attract more female talent in the field. Whatever it is, focusing on the benchmark as opposed to a quota provides you with flexibility and a way to identify areas to troubleshoot. The same approach can be applied to hiring and promoting of ethnic minorities. If your office is based in a city or a country where ethnic minorities make up, say, 33% of the population, yet your workforce has less than 10% of its workforce from that demographic, then again, there is clearly something going on. The answer isn't to then force the organisation to instantly meet a quota, but instead deep dive into the issues and provide more foundational solutions.

Having said this, there is one solution that is superior to all other solutions when it comes to ensuring more female and minority talent make it into both the organisation and leadership ranks. It is also a really obvious solution. It is to implement a proper objective, fact-based assessment process for both hiring and managing performance. This is undoubtedly the easiest way to ensure a more diverse leadership team. If a selection process assesses an individual based on their abilities, performance, results, management style, and so on, you are going to end up with more women in leadership roles. This is the honest reality about companies with a higher proportion of female or minority leaders who have proved successful. They often have not had quotas, but they have had strong leadership assessment capabilities. It's why they were already in the lead before this subject of leadership diversity became mainstream. They made a female or a minority the CEO, CFO or COO, etc., because they were clearly the best person for the job, and everyone in the company knew it.

It has been repeatedly proven that objective as opposed to subjective assessments lead to more diverse candidates being both hired and promoted. Imagine an objective assessment for promoting someone that operated more like an academic exam. You could not just promote Rick over Sally and Rajesh because the boss thought Rick had more leadership potential. Instead, this claim has to be backed up with substantive evidence that proves beyond doubt that Rick is more deserving. This means they would need to collate psychometric leadership assessment scores, peer reviewed feedback of performance, testimonials, and other evidence-based performance feedback. It is hard to argue that

Rick deserves to be promoted over Sally or Rajesh if Rick has lower scores on his leadership assessment test and both Sally and Rajesh's teams delivered every project ahead of schedule while all of Rick's projects were delayed. Even more damning, imagine if, on top of this, Rick's team attrition rate is 32% while Sally's is 12%, and Rajesh's is 18%.

If a business can accurately assess leadership capability, research has already shown that women generally score higher than men in 17 of 19 leadership skills. There is a great study from Harvard Business Review that backs this up. This is because the traits that make a great leader are predominantly soft skills. For example, the ability to display empathy, coach and mentor, support and guide, balance competing priorities (multi-tasking), and so on, are areas where women consistently outscore men. There are also numerous ways to assess such things in an objective, fact-based, evidence-led way. The old-fashioned alpha male, who dominates and asserts and gets aggressive when pressed, is incapable of scoring high in an impartial, objective capability-based assessment. Therefore, if an organisation can implement a full comprehensive performance-based assessment, a natural outcome of that would be for more women and minorities to make it through to leadership positions.

Chapter 3: Goal Setting

If you want to create an organisation that delivers a great employee experience, enables a culture of high engagement and high performance, and generally ensures the organisation is a success, then you have to be able to set effective goals for employees. You read that right. Goal setting is the key to everything. Unfortunately, many managers and some HR teams treat it like a once-a-year admin exercise, but it is actually one of the most important ingredients of success. Your ability to motivate, engage and retain employees, as well as hit all of your organisational deliverables, are dependent on being able to set proper goals for the whole team. Despite goal setting being a critical foundational requirement for successfully leading teams, most in management neglect this exercise and deem it as not important. Very few understand that this failure is the reason that when the end of the year arrives, deliverables have not been hit, the team are disengaged, and their top performer wants to quit. Quite simply, the goals a manager sets for the team will shape everything their team does throughout the year.

At its most basic level, the reason goal setting is so important is because it shapes the priorities employees are going to devote their attention to. Think about this from a member of staff's perspective. What do you think they will spend most of their time focused on—activities that directly impact their performance review and the pay rise and bonus they will receive or activities that have no bearing on the level of pay rise or bonus they will receive? The answer is, of course, incredibly self-evident, as

99.99% of the population are going to focus on what directly benefits them the most. This is why goal setting is so critical to high performance and engagement. In fact, whenever high performers are profiled, they are consistently shown as being very goal oriented. For an organisation, goal setting is the primary weapon in your arsenal to align the employees to the right goals for maximum impact. How you set those goals will go a long way to deciding whether your teams are directionless throughout the year or if they are going all out to deliver exceptional results.

Effective goal setting provides your people with a clearly defined purpose. There is a huge difference in engagement and performance levels of those simply performing a job as opposed to those aligned to working towards a much larger purpose. So, if you are able to get goal setting right, you will infuse your employees with a clear reason why they are coming in to work every day. If you fail to do this, they are merely turning up for a pay cheque because they have bills to pay. But if they are aligned to delivering a much larger purpose, they are more likely to put in more hours and push a lot harder to deliver exceptional outcomes. This is why purpose and engagement levels are seen as being so closely linked. The more aligned a member of staff is to help deliver on a purpose that is beyond just their own job, the higher their levels of engagement. The higher their levels of engagement, the higher the level of performance and motivation of the team, and the less likely it is that the team will resign. You also have the benefit of being able to refresh the goals each year, so if you get it right, this will allow you to constantly have an employee base that is highly engaged and driven to outperform.

The goals you set for your employees will also play a large part in how the culture of the company develops. If you are trying to build a culture of innovation, but everyone's goals are linked to the same KPIs they have always been linked to, it is unlikely the employees are going to feel the need to do anything differently. For example, if you were to set a goal of ensuring 90% of customer interactions are responded to within 24 hours and the team consistently get close to this mark, that is not going to be seen as a sign that the team need to change anything drastically. Even if the team do not get close to the mark, they will still not see this as a sign that they need to innovate. If they typically only respond to 25% of customer interactions in that time period, their response is likely to be that they need more headcount, not innovative ways of working. If goal setting is done properly, it will build the culture your company requires.

So, rather than setting the same old KPIs and hoping for innovation, it would be wiser to set a goal for each employee to change/improve at least one process this year. This will ensure that the employees direct their attention to where you want it to be—after all, it is through innovation and change that you will improve results, not just by simply adding more headcount to do things how they have always been done. The same is true of other aspects of company culture and the link to goal setting. If everyone is rewarded on an individual basis, then why would they care about collaboration, or if a person in the team is not performing? Whereas if their performance outcomes are tied into ensuring the whole team succeeds, not just them, then they are likely to take the time to collaborate and help others.

For goal setting to be effective, achieving or failing to deliver on goals must also be consequential. One of the reasons the annual goal-setting process is so ineffectual is because, at year-end, it rarely seems to matter. Not only do managers and HR fail to set proper goals for the team, but when it comes to performance assessment, they are often not really factored into year-end outcomes. So, if you are a member of staff who exceeds all expectations and doesn't get a promotion or a good pay rise at the end of the year, then why would you care about achieving your goals moving forward? Why would you do all of that extra work when you received the same pay rise as you did last year when you did the bare minimum? Likewise, if you fail to achieve your goals and still get a pay rise and a bonus, why should you worry about taking on all of that extra work? If there is no consequence to a person's pay or career prospects one way or another, then the whole exercise is pointless. And as we have discussed, goal setting should be far from a pointless exercise if you want to create a high performing team. Without it, your employees will end up meandering through and delivering mediocre results, and you will be left wondering why business results are stagnating and the workforce is disengaged.

Setting Goals

Ok, so we are clear on why goals are important for your employees and organisation, but how should you go about setting them? The first step is to actually avoid making the mistake that most organisations make when setting goals for their employees. This is to set goals that, in reality, are business as usual activities.

The goals you set for your employees are the standards you expect from them. So, if you have an accountant who works for your company and you set a goal for them to do the accounts, this isn't an effective goal. An accountant completing the year-end accounts is the bare minimum they would need to do to keep their job. This isn't a high-performance objective; it is a minimum requirement. If your accountant is not completing the year-end accounts, then you need to fire them. If they are completing the year-end accounts, this isn't a reason to celebrate them being a high achiever; it is the absolute minimum expectation of their employment. Likewise, your customer service person 'effectively dealing with customer queries' is not a goal; it's also a minimum expectation of their employment. If you have a payroll person, ensuring the payroll is processed is not a goal, it is the minimum expectation of their job. The whole reason they are employed is to process payroll. It is the equivalent of businesses giving awards and recognition for 100% attendance. It reinforces the belief that the bare minimum—turning up to work—is an achievement. This is not how you create a high engagement and performance organisation that will achieve great things.

To use goal setting to create a high-performance organisation, you need to set high performance goals. This means that instead of asking your accountant to prepare the year-end accounts, you set them a goal of improving the financial reporting process to reduce the time it takes to prepare the accounts. This forces them to think beyond what they have always done and find new ways of working to improve the speed at which the accounts are prepared. This will result in a more efficient accounting process, leading to a more efficient finance team that will deliver better results. This then means that your organisation is more efficient and has a stronger finance team which in turn will improve performance for the business as a whole. This approach is something that can be taken to literally any type of role within your company—you are only limited by your imagination. Your payroll person can have a goal of finding a better payroll system. A customer service agent can be asked to come up with a scheme to improve customer satisfaction levels. This will shift the employees' approach from performing tasks because it's their job to do them and focusing on improving performance.

As you go through this process of goal setting, it is also important to remember to ensure the goals you are setting are aligned to the company's overall strategy. There is very little logic in having your sales team focus on generating new international sales if the organisation is focused on growing its domestic market share. Likewise, there is very little point in having the team focus on new domestic clients if the aim is to expand internationally. Look to the organisational strategy and values for direction. If your organisation is looking to develop new ways of working and becoming more digital, agile, or innovative, that will give you a clear direction as to what you should be doing with your employees. You then need to translate that into each team and find proactive ways for your employees to contribute to them.

The trick to having employees buy into the goals and go all out to deliver on them is to have them feel like they have ownership and accountability for the goals. One of the easiest ways to do this is to have employees come up with their own goals, and then HR and the manager guide and coach them to get them to where they need to be. There is nothing more powerful than a member of staff trying to deliver on their own idea. There is a huge difference in engagement between a member of staff delivering something because their boss has told them that they need to do it and doing it because they personally believe that it will have a big impact on the organisation. The feeling that the idea belongs to them and that they are empowered to implement it is a strong one. By simply asking your employees what they can do to improve performance, you will be amazed at the ideas they will come up with. Salespeople will volunteer to make more sales calls and conduct more meetings, and operational members of staff will proactively suggest processes and systems that should be streamlined. A little bit of ownership and involving employees in the process of deciding the priorities will go a long way.

Short-Term Goals

A good employee experience is not dependent on the workplace being fun. There is no need for the facilities management team to rush out and buy bean bag chairs and pool tables and ensure that every Tuesday is Tequila Tuesday. Don't get me wrong; that might sound kind of fun, or at least would have when I was in my twenties, but none of this is essential to a great employee experience. Instead, research consistently shows that a positive employee experience is tied into employees finding meaning and purpose in their work, impacting the organization, and receiving real-time feedback and appreciation for their contribution. It is proven that the majority of employees would stay with an organisation if they felt fairly paid and well treated, even if they knew they could get more money elsewhere. It is also shown that there is a less than 1% chance of employees becoming disengaged due to negative feedback as long as they feel their strengths are also appreciated. Despite all of this, many organisations fail to utilise basic yet meaningful ways to achieve this in favour of superficial activities such as setting up a pool table in the breakout area. Whilst a pool table can be fun, it does not help an employee find meaning in their work, have an impact on an organisation or receive appreciation for their contribution. There is, however, an incredibly simple and free approach that can provide employees with these essentials. This approach is to provide employees with meaningful short-term goals.

When goal setting is typically discussed and implemented within an organisation there is a natural focus to set goals for the year. This is understandable because performance is managed one year at a time. So, an organisation will naturally set goals for the year so they can manage performance and help identify who should be promoted or given a good pay rise for the work they have done in the previous year. However, this approach can be flawed because it is rarely implemented well. We have already discussed how focusing on promotions as a reward for doing a good job last year negatively impacts a company. But there are other ways in which annual goal setting can create disengagement when not implemented properly. The primary issues revolve around real-time recognition and immediacy of outcomes.

A really easy example would be to assume someone needs to improve a process this year. If they implement the changes by the end of July, what are they meant to be focused on for the rest of the year? They have completed their objectives, so now they are left directionless until new goals are set for next year. This means that for the next 5 months, they are just going to be performing a normal business as usual role, completing various tasks, and so on. This is a huge problem because research shows that employees are more likely to quit if they are bored as opposed to overworked. They crave engagement and purpose, and if they aren't being provided with that, then they will look elsewhere. In addition, because of the nature of the annual performance review, they completed their objectives in July but are going to have to wait until December to have their performance reviewed and recognised. This is the equivalent of watching your child do a cartwheel for the first time and not saying anything and then 5 months later, at Christmas, congratulating them on doing a cartwheel. You might have recognised it, but it just doesn't mean as much.

This is why short-term goals should be a cornerstone of any employee experience and engagement strategy. It is the only way to provide a continuous purpose to your employees. Keeping your job by doing what your boss asks you any given day isn't a purpose. A purpose is very much about ensuring your employees are motivated and keen to come into work every day because they are trying to achieve important things. This is also another often-overlooked benefit of Agile. Within an organisation running on Agile principles, they will often break down big pieces of work into a series of smaller objectives called sprints. The easiest way to think about this is to imagine you are working on a project for 18 months. Rather than focusing on it as one big piece of work that is only completed when everything is done— and let's be honest, such big projects always run into delays—the project would be broken down into 18 one-month sprints. This means that the project operates as 18 mini projects as opposed to one big one. This approach usually results in a project being delivered more efficiently than the larger traditional projects (which always get delayed) because there are a short-term focus, milestones, and goals to be delivered each month. This means the team are consistently energised to tick off the next accomplishment. They have a purpose they are working towards, and when they complete that mini project, the next one starts straight away.

Without these short-term objectives, your employees are simply turning up for work because they are required to do so in order to keep their jobs. There is nothing specific or important they are working towards. So, all they are doing is performing a list of tasks their boss has told them to do in return for their salary. That is the only reason they are in the office. Hence, if someone else phones them up and offers them more money to perform those same tasks elsewhere, they will accept it because why would they turn it down? There is no more significant reason for them to stay. They have no purpose, no important objectives or goals they are working for; they are merely working a job. Therefore, if someone else wants to offer them more money, then, of course, they are going to take it. They would be stupid not to. But if an employee has a clear sense of what they are trying to achieve and why it is important to the organisation, they are much more likely to stay. Short-term goals are perfect for providing this.

In addition to providing a purpose, there is another tangible benefit to providing consistent short-term goals to your employees—they feel like they are succeeding. Short-term goals enable a positive employee experience and an increase in engagement because it provides employees with a sense of accomplishment. Rather than waiting for the year-end review or for 18 months if we were to use the 18-month project example, they are able to consistently complete objectives. This means they will constantly feel like they are achieving something of note. They will know they are performing well, contributing positively to the organisation, and have a sense of purpose and belonging. Short-term goals theoretically allow for this to exist in perpetuity because the nature of short-term goals means they can be created in a way that is a continuous cycle. One of the best ways to ensure this type of thing thrives throughout the organisation is to focus on building a culture of continuous improvement. This means there will always be something for an employee to work on and drive high levels of performance and engagement. One of the easiest ways to begin this process would be to ask employees to come up with one way to improve their ways of working each quarter. This would provide a never-ending list of objectives and, therefore, a never-ending list of achievements and contributions. It would also spur growth and development within teams as they look to keep up to date with the latest innovations and tools to help create new ideas. This means they are always going to feel like they have some meaningful work to do that is delivering an impact.

The other major benefit of short-term goals is that it provides employees with something they consistently say they want—feedback. Research has repeatedly shown that consistent real-time feedback is a critical component of both employee experience and engagement. It is also something that research shows is consistently lacking in management. A significant number of employees only have one performance-related conversation with their manager outside of the year-end review. This is a key reason why only 14% of employees report that the year-end review motivates them to perform well. If someone does a great job on delivering a project in February, they want to be told they did a good job in February, not in December when they are doing the annual performance review. Likewise, if they didn't do a great job in February on that project, they would like to know what they could have done better and coached to improve that area in February too. Short-term goals enable a culture where performance and feedback have to occur more regularly. This, in turn, boosts engagement and creates a more positive employee experience.

Long-Term Goals

While short-term goals are incredibly effective at improving engagement and employee experience, they are, of course, not a solution on their own. This is why it is important to combine short-term goals with much longer-term goals that will go beyond the traditional one-year performance management cycle. This is because there is an important nuance in employee engagement and experience that is often overlooked. The organisation has to provide an employee with a reason to want to stick around for the longer term. Short-term goals naturally provide a short-term reason for an employee to stick around, and it's an extremely powerful tool to boost engagement and experience. But there has to be some sort of reward or career development for an employee long term, otherwise, why would they stay? Sure, they are working on some cool projects and achieving some cool things, but at some point, an employee is going to begin to ask—what is in it for me? Sure, they are delivering some great outcomes for the organisation, but if they do not also benefit from it, why would they want to stick around for the longer term? So, it is important to remember that purpose is a two-way street.

This means there are two elements of purpose and meaningful work. There is the element of purpose being that people want to work on important work that has meaning, but it also has to benefit them in the longer term. Otherwise, there is no purpose for them to remain with your company. They don't have a career; they have a job. So, if someone wants to pay them more to perform that job elsewhere, they will eventually take it. So, if you do not provide an employee with a reason to still be with the organisation in 3 years' time, then the likelihood is that they will not be with the organisation in 3 years' time. This is why long-term goals are also incredibly important. You can't build a great employee experience and have sustainable high engagement for the long term if there are no long-term objectives.

One of the easiest ways for an organisation to provide engaging long-term goals relates to providing its employees with new skills and experiences. Employee development is critical to ensuring long-term engagement and retention. After all, without this, there is no reason for the employee to stick around long term. In addition, employee development is literally in everyone's best interest. The company wins because it means its employees are going to be more highly skilled and, therefore, able to deliver more valuable outcomes for the business. Likewise, the employee wins because they are gaining new skills and experiences, allowing them to develop their own career. This kind of long-term goal becomes the glue holding all of the short-term goals together. Thus, creating a dynamic where there is consistent short-term high performance combined with long-term purpose and engagement. An example from my own personal experience of doing this would relate to an administrator who worked for me in a previous role. This administrator was in their 50s and had only ever performed admin-related roles. This person was provided with a number of short-term goals to automate the majority of administrative processes over the following two years in a series of short-term sprints. This was combined with a longer-term goal of providing them with the skills to manage automation transformations and then manage the systems and tools that were put in place as part of the transition. This provided the person with some really interesting short-term deliverables and combined them with longer-term capability development.

The cherry on top of the cake regarding long-term goal setting is combining all of this with career growth. Every project, training session, and piece of work should be aligned to delivering on an eventual promotion or sideways move into another department. This is obviously not possible on an annual basis, but basic talent management and succession planning work should be aligned to not expecting any employee to stay in a role for more than three years. It is pretty common for employees to change roles every 3 years, and the average tenure of employees around the world, regardless of geography, industry, specialism, and so on, shows that 3 years is usually the tipping point. The reason for this is simple. In year one, an employee is learning their new position and getting to know their surroundings. In year two, they are excelling and improving in the role. Then in year three, the mind naturally begins to wonder what is next. After all, very few employees want to just spend the next 10, 20, 30, or more years doing the same thing. They want to grow, develop, earn more money, provide a better life for their families, and so on. In order to do this, they must be able to grow their career. So, if they are not doing this with your organisation, then they will be doing it elsewhere.

SMART Goals

OK, we have covered why goals are important and how the best way to create a great employee experience and high levels of engagement and performance is to combine short-term and long-term goals. So, how do we set effective goals? The good news is that when it comes to setting effective goals, there is a ready-made template to ensure the goal meets a high standard. This template or method is known as SMART. A SMART goal is essentially a best-in-class methodology to help guide goal setting. It has become popular with HR and corporate organisations as a whole and is often the go-to methodology of many organisations that have a structured goal-setting process. SMART is an acronym that stands for Specific, Measurable, Achievable, Relevant, and Timely. Therefore, a SMART goal incorporates all of these criteria to help create clarity and focus, increasing the chances of achieving the goal. It is also a method you can use for other personal goals outside of work. To understand how you can ensure that the goals you set for employees within the organisation are SMART goals, you can use the following as a guide:

Specific: The starting point for any goal should be that the goal is well defined, clear, and unambiguous. Goals that are specific have a significantly greater chance of being accomplished than those that aren't. In fact, one of the reasons why most 'goals' are not achieved is because they are not really goals. For example, being rich is not a goal. Creating a marketing business that generates a profit of $10 million a year is a goal. Likewise, within a professional setting, simply doing more sales or some other sort of activity is not a goal. It is vague and unclear. So, asking your salesperson to sell more next year is not a specific goal. If they sell $1 more than last year, they will have technically achieved the goal, but I guarantee you that the management team didn't mean to sell $1 more. However, setting a specific goal of selling an additional 15% on top of last year by going after a specific new market segment is a clear goal. For an operational person, rather than asking them to improve a process, the goal would be set to identify a specific pain point that needs to be addressed, and that process should be the one they need to improve. One of the easiest ways to ensure a goal is specific is to use the 5 W's. Define who is involved in the goal, what they need to accomplish, where it will be accomplished, when it should be achieved by, and why that is important. To cap it off and close the loop, you should also cover specifically how it will be achieved.

Measurable: In addition to being specific, a goal must also have criteria for measuring progress. If there are no measurable criteria, then you will not be able to determine if someone is on track to reach their goal. Ultimately, this is the whole point of doing goal setting. You want to ensure the team are measured on performance, and to do this, you have to be able to measure that performance effectively and objectively. If a goal is not measurable, then you will not be able to assess performance. It is this lack of measurability that often leads to uncomfortable year-end performance conversations between a manager and their staff. If your performance goals are measurable, then there should be absolutely no doubt as to whether someone has failed to meet expectations, met expectations, or exceeded them. If you were to set a perfect set of goals, a 10-year-old should be able to do your team's year-end assessments because the outcomes should be that obvious. But this is only possible if the goals are clearly measurable.

When setting the criteria, you should always aim to focus on outcomes as opposed to activities. For example, your sales staff may have a series of KPIs such as making 100 phone calls a day or conducting 5 meetings a week. But if their sales target is to make $100,000 in a year, that should be the overall measurable criteria. Many businesses get this wrong, though, and will actually tell someone who has sold $250,000 against a $100,000 target that they underperformed because they didn't make enough phone calls. This is, of course, complete idiocy, but unfortunately, common sense is not that common, and this kind of thing happens more often than it should. That same manager and business are then shocked when that person quits 3 months later and desperately try to retain them. For objectives that have less clear financial metrics, such as improving a process, you should focus on the overall delivery date. There may be a lengthy plan with a series of milestones to ensure delivery. But again, as long as it is delivered in the required timelines, in the grand scheme of things, it really shouldn't matter if every other milestone had some sort of hiccup. When it comes to process improvements, and especially those with tech dependencies, hiccups are to be expected.

Achievable: It is also essential for the goal to be achievable and attainable. If it is not, then it is not a fair goal. Providing an employee with a goal that is not achievable is an easy way to demotivate them and lead to them becoming disengaged quickly. After all, why would they bother to put in a huge effort to do something they believe is impossible—especially if their end-of-year performance review and bonus are dependent on it. Rather than delivering high performance, you are more likely to deliver high attrition. An easy example of an unachievable goal is to expect a sales employee who was the top performer and sold $100,000 last year to sell $100,000,000 this year. It is, of course, completely unrealistic to expect this to happen. At the same time, it may also be unrealistic to expect them to sell $100,000 every month. Likewise, if your business has also cut the price of your product from $100 to $25, then expecting them to hit $100,000 again would also be unrealistic as you are essentially asking them to sell four times as much as last year. For non-sales staff, asking your customer service person to deal with 900 customers a day instead of 90 could be another example. As would implementing a piece of technology that normally takes 9 months in 9 weeks.

While all of this seems obvious, many think that big, bold goals will inspire the team, but when it comes to performance assessment, they don't. This doesn't mean there should not be big, bold goals; it just means they shouldn't be part of the annual goal-setting exercise. There is nothing wrong with aspiring to get from $100,000 to $100,000,000 or tech implementations down from 9 months to 9 weeks, but if you tie a person's annual bonus and promotion chances to achieving that within the next 12 months, you will lose the team. These big, bold goals should be seen as the cherry on top of the cake rather than the cake itself. As an example, Elon Musk once lost an incredibly talented member of staff because she knew there was absolutely no way to deliver on a goal of delivering 100,000 cars in a quarter. She knew it was possible, at best, to get to circa 80,000 at that point in the company's journey. They simply did not have the logistics in place to deliver more in such a short time frame, and having led logistics within the US Military, she kind of knew what she was talking about. She left the company after a big argument with Musk, and at the end of the quarter, the team delivered just over 80,000 deliveries. This was a milestone that Musk himself celebrated as an amazing achievement once it was delivered, yet by keeping the goal at 100,000 when it was impossible, he lost an incredibly talented member of staff.

Relevant: When setting goals, they should also be relevant. In the context of goals for your employees, this means both relevant to the company and relevant to the member of staff. For example, tying your receptionist's year-end performance review into the performance of the sales team is stupid, but many organisations make this mistake. The year-end bonus pool is, of course, dependent on the financial performance of the organisation, but the individual performance of each member of staff is not. Therefore, when setting goals, it is important to ensure the goals for your employees are relevant to areas they are able to directly influence. If it is not, the employee will become disengaged and demotivated as they will not be able to influence the outcome of their performance review. If they lose out on a promotion because someone in another team who has nothing to do with their work underperformed, then they are going to quit. Asking a salesperson to improve the process between sales and finance so that invoices are issued faster may be relevant if there is a lot of documentation required, such as customer details, etc., that sales are responsible for gathering. However, asking the sales team to ensure that the finance team process the payments faster is not something that is relevant as they do not have control of the finance team's internal process. This should be a goal for the finance team themselves. In addition, the goal should not only be relevant to what the member of staff themselves can influence, but the goal should also be relevant to the company strategy. For example, there is little point in trying to expand internationally if the strategy is to expand domestically or vice versa. It doesn't mean there isn't an opportunity there; it just means the team should be focused on the strategic aims of the organisation.

Timely: Finally, a goal must be time-bound. This means that it has a start and end date. Quite simply, if the goal is not time-constrained, there will be no sense of urgency or way to measure it. As such, there must be a clear and reasonable timeline for achieving the goal. Given the nature of performance assessments following the same timelines as an organisation's financial year, the goals should consist of things that can be delivered within the 12 months of the assessment year. If something is going to take longer than 12 months, then you will need to break it down into more manageable bite-size pieces so that it fits into the performance assessment cycle. For longer-term development goals, such as a promotion in 3 years' time, this would also be broken down into shorter-term metrics to ensure all is on track. So, for example, a person must complete a training course and pass the exam in Q2 in order to then work on a project in Q3. They would then deliver the big project in 18 months' time, at which point they would be promoted and, in the interim, have a number of smaller deliverables that feed into that.

Chapter 4: Motivation & Recognition

In the years I have spent coaching leaders and advising organisations, one of the questions I am always asked is how they can motivate their staff. I lost count a long time ago as to how many times I have been asked this question—it is that common. It is also a question that always makes me chuckle. There always seems to be this belief that there is some secret trick that, when used by a manager or a member of HR, will magically boost motivation, productivity, and engagement by 700% and eliminate all employee attrition and dissatisfaction instantly. The truth is that there is a secret trick to achieving all of this, but it isn't usually the answer they want to hear. The answer is to ensure you have a high level of management capability, as outlined in Chapter 2 of this book. As I have shared in both this book and others, while a manager isn't the only cause of employee attrition, they are the leading cause by a long way. Before a member of staff resigns, they first become disengaged and demotivated. It is an endless cycle, but one that can be positively influenced. Just as employee attrition is a sign of bad management, low attrition is a sign of good management. The impact of a manager is so significant that research has shown that almost 40% of employees would rather do unpleasant work than sit next to a micromanager. When almost half of your employees say they would rather do something they dislike than sit next to a bad manager, the message is very clear.

Let me ask you a question. How many times have you woken up in the morning and thought, '*Hmm, I am going to intentionally do a terrible job today. I don't want a promotion or a pay rise, and I think it will be fun to be really difficult with my boss and colleagues*? I am assuming it is none. The same is true of your employees. The truth is that all employees are motivated and keen to do well. They want to do a good job. They want to succeed in their role. They want to secure a promotion and a pay rise. They want to have positive relationships with their colleagues. They want to work for the company and perform their role—otherwise, they wouldn't have accepted an offer to join the company in the first place and would have already resigned as well. Ironically, it is often their manager or the organisational leadership as a whole who demotivates them—leading to many negative outcomes. To successfully keep a team engaged and motivated, rather than trying to push them to be motivated, the best organisations instead focus on not demotivating the team. They understand that their people want to succeed, and so it is their job to ensure they are providing the team with the right environment and support to do so.

The path to achieving this begins with goal setting, as we have outlined in the previous chapter. After all, this is foundational to the entire purpose of all of your employees being with the company in the first place. Assuming you get the goal-setting piece right, then you are off to a good start. But from there, the engagement and motivation of your team are entirely dependent on how their managers conduct themselves combined with the support and official programmes set up by the HR department. This doesn't mean that management and HR should be pushovers who never provide any constructive or negative feedback in case you upset someone. But it does mean you need to be mindful of the actions of the manager in particular. According to research, the manager's behaviour is going to be directly responsible for 70% of employees' engagement levels. This is through their day-to-day interactions with the team, discussion about their team's career development, the culture of both the team and the organisation as a whole, and the way the organisation measure and reward performance, along with the level of salary and benefits staff receive, among other things.

So, where does HR come into this? I have obviously spent a lot of time emphasising how management capability is the biggest variable when defining employee experience and engagement. The HR department's role in this is essential to fill the gap in between. Many people consider an organisation to be split into two groups. There is the management group and the wider employee base. But, to deliver a great employee experience, high levels of engagement and business performance in an organisation should consist of three pillars. There is the management group, the wider employee base, and also the HR department. The role of HR should be seen not as part of one or the other but rather as the champion and protector of the organisational environment as a whole. It is the HR department's responsibility to identify the gaps and challenges preventing its people from reaching their maximum output and put in place programmes to both support and compensate for this.

If a manager lacks the required capability, it is HR's job to ensure there is a management training programme, and the manager is also receiving ongoing coaching and advice to ensure they make the right decisions related to getting the most out of their people. If a manager wants to promote the wrong member of staff, it is on HR to ensure the promotion criteria are clear and helps the manager come to the right conclusion. If a manager isn't recognising their people, HR should create a recognition programme that forces a manager to regularly nominate someone in their team to be recognised. Likewise, if a member of staff is failing despite the manager doing an amazing job at trying to support the employee, then HR would step in and provide access to a training and development programme or some other kinds of support to help the employee succeed. It is a crucial role, and without a strategic HR department providing this support, an organisation will never be able to maintain an environment of high engagement and motivation that delivers outstanding business results consistently.

Recognition

The mistake many in management and HR make when the topic of recognition comes up is to instantly assume it must be financial. It isn't. Recognition is something that is able to be given every single day and, in most cases, it's free. This is because the path to disengagement and demotivation begins by failing to recognise the good work the team are doing each and every day. Research has shown that there is only a 1% chance of an employee becoming disengaged if they feel their strengths are recognised. The harsh truth is that most of us in management and HR take the good work that our people do for granted and, most of the time, only discuss the things that are going wrong. It is fine to provide constructive feedback when a mistake is made, providing that you also recognise the other dozen things that the person does well. This doesn't mean that before you criticise someone, you praise them (this is actually not that effective, as I will explain later in this book). It means that when they complete a piece of work, recognise it. Depending on the work, it could be a simple 'well done', it could be an email to them or the whole team, it could be buying them a coffee or taking them out to lunch, it could even be letting them come in an hour later the next day or going home early. But it is important that the staff feel that the organisation is seeing the good work they do. If this does not happen, then the staff are going to feel that all their boss or company does is call out their mistakes. No positive relationship can be built, whether personal or professional, by consistently pointing out flaws with no sort of positive reinforcement in between. It might be a few days, weeks, months, or years, but eventually, that relationship is going to break down.

Remember, motivation is not something you can do to anyone. You can demotivate them, but you can't actually motivate them to do more. Motivation can only come from the person themselves. People choose when to go the extra mile and give their all. You can only create an environment that may or may not result in people choosing to be motivated. So, ask yourself a question—when would a person choose to work extra hours late one evening or over the weekend to get something awesome delivered? Are they going to choose to do this if they never get any recognition for the effort they put in? Are they more likely to choose to do so if they know it will be appreciated and recognised? The day-to-day interactions between employees and their manager, along with support from formal programmes from the organisation, will set the stage for whether or not they choose to be motivated enough to go that extra mile when you need the team to deliver. Research shows that, more often than not, the majority of managers aren't doing this effectively. Another Gartner study shows that only 21% of employees think their performance is managed and measured in a way that motivates them to do well. Or, to put it another way, 79% of employees think, *why should I bother? Because I am not going to be recognised for it anyway.*

A famous quote from Maya Angelou says that people will forget specifically what you said or did, but they will always remember how you made them feel. It is also a quote that perfectly encapsulates the impact of recognition on staff and why there is such a disconnect between managers and HR teams who feel they are doing something and staff who say they are not. If you had a spouse who made you feel awful all of the time, even though they said they loved you, would you stick around? Of course, you wouldn't. The same is true of your staff when it comes to their relationship with the organisation. Regardless of what you think you are doing, if your employees do not feel like you appreciate them, they will not be engaged and motivated.

The most authentic recognition is real-time recognition. Let me ask you a question. If you had a child who did a cartwheel for the first time or got top marks in an exam or an equivalent achievement, would you wait until their next birthday or the next public holiday, such as Christmas, Chinese New Year, or Diwali, to recognise their achievement? Of course not. It would be utterly ridiculous. Yet, in the corporate world, management and HR do the equivalent of this all of the time. They will wait until the formal review or a company event of some sort before recognising staff. Think about how this looks logically from an employee's point of view. They worked hard and won a new client or streamlined a process. Then at some point, a few weeks or months later, they have it acknowledged with a certificate or an email or everyone clapping at the next town hall. It's just so fake and inauthentic. By then, the moment has passed, and all of the pride and enthusiasm of the employee is gone. In fact, they have probably spent the last few weeks or months feeling unappreciated for that good thing they have achieved as no one has recognised it. So, when it is finally recognised later, it doesn't mean as much.

This is a key reason why many official corporate employee recognition programmes fail to deliver the expected results. It's not because employees are against the idea of being recognised formally by the organisation, but it needs to be done in tandem with real-time recognition from the manager. Waiting 4 months to congratulate your child on doing their first cartwheel or getting top marks in an exam would be meaningless because 4 months later, they will have done a load more cartwheels and/or taken more exams. They won't appreciate it as much. But recognising them in the moment for their achievement as a proud parent will mean more, and taking them to the zoo or Disneyworld a few months later as a formal celebration is a great bonus. This is what you need to aim for with your own employee recognition programmes. They want to know you see and appreciate the good things they are doing, and if there is also an extra formal recognition as part of the organisation as well, that is the cherry on top of the cake.

HR are able to play a vital role in bridging the gap between employees who feel they are not being recognised and a management group that may or may not care about providing recognition. This is best done by setting up a series of formal and informal programmes and solutions to ensure the issue is addressed and staff are recognised. However, it is important that when this is done, steps are taken to avoid some of the most common reasons why these types of programmes fail. The truth is that most formal recognition programmes fail for one of two reasons. The first is that management simply don't participate. A recognition programme is typically set up in response to employees feeling like they lack recognition. But the reason they lack recognition is because their managers aren't recognising them. Therefore, HR set up a programme that will allow for managers to recognise them, but the managers simply continue not to recognise them. The second reason is that the programme is seen as fake, insincere, and generally inauthentic. Just as office parties and events can be terrible because organised fun is very rarely fun, recognition programmes can suffer the same fate. Organised praise can rarely seem authentic, especially if the programme is seen as a simple box-ticking exercise.

The role of HR is to bridge the gap between what the organisation and its people need and what the management team has the capability to deliver. It is, therefore, incredibly important that any HR-sponsored or supported recognition programme begins with the aim of encouraging and enabling managers to deliver real-time recognition. Without this, everything else will seem superficial. After all, employee experience is the experience of an employee's day to day employment. So, if their boss is not recognising the good, it doesn't matter if there is a formal recognition programme run by HR; their experience will be that they are not appreciated for the work they do. This requires some proactive outreach from HR to ensure it is successful, as in most organisations, this is a domain that is often just left to managers—which is why the problem is so profound. Managers often have no idea who or what to recognise. This means a great starting point is to put together a framework or guide of some sort to help managers understand what they should praise and how. This may seem unnecessary, and that it should be obvious, but research consistently shows that it is needed. This research isn't just backed up by employees saying they want to be recognised, but significant amounts of research show managers themselves want more support and guidance in handling these day-to-day people-management interactions. This is because they have never been shown how to behave in such circumstances. There is very little management training focused on what to do if you need to ask a member of staff to work late, for example. The guide should cover a spectrum of recognition from saying thank you and good job for completing simple tasks to potentially allowing staff to start work later the following day if they worked late to meet an unexpected critical deliverable.

So, if a senior leader needs an urgent report at short notice—a very common occurrence that leads to a middle manager and their team needing to flounder around and find some data and put together a couple of slides—the person who ends up having to send the final version over at 11 pm at night could be given the morning off as a thank you. Alternatively, the manager could take those individuals who needed to work late out for lunch the following day or something similar. The guide should cover various other scenarios too, and essentially act as a playbook the managers can refer to when it comes to working out how to respond appropriately to ensure the member of staff feels their contribution has been recognised. In addition, some budget could be set aside for the manager to pay for things such as coffees, lunches, some gift cards, etc., that they can give out as required when staff achieve certain things of note that deserve more than just a quick thank you or well done.

The programme's effectiveness can then be monitored through a few different methods. The budget spend can be monitored, so if managers aren't using the budget, then you know they are not recognising people. You could also ask the managers to self-report on recognition activities they have done each week and also run a regular survey for employees to see if they report they are being recognised. The survey approach can seem daunting because a huge amount of work goes into engagement surveys, but something such as this could simply be run via SurveyMonkey and kept to a simple yes or no question format to ensure reporting is easy. This will then allow for interventions with managers who are clearly not prioritising recognition of their people day to day.

Once the foundational pillar of enabling real-time recognition from managers is completed, this is when it is time to add all of the fancy bells and whistles to the organisational recognition programme. The more conventional programmes should be broken down into informal and formal recognition. Informal recognition programmes that the HR department would enable would be things such as setting up a Slack channel or social media hashtag to encourage those in the organisation to recognise the work of others in the company. The aim would be to create a culture where employees naturally begin to recognise the contributions of each other. So, if someone has an issue with their laptop and IT Helpdesk helps them out, they should then head over to the Slack channel or social media and shout them out for their assistance. This usually works better on Slack or other internal communication tools as opposed to social media, but depending on the culture and industry, it does work on social media too.

It may take a little while for employees to begin to participate as it is likely to be a cultural shift, so it may help to provide some incentives and encouragement. This might be as simple as posting on Slack, 'Hey, team, we have a $20 Starbucks gift card to give away—who in the team do you feel is deserving of it for their contributions this week?' This will help slowly shift the culture and then combine this with sending out communications to managers to ensure they shout out at least one person in their team each week on the channel to help get the ball rolling. Sharing a little report of which managers did and didn't recognise people on Slack each week/month to the leadership team will also help nudge the culture in the right direction. If you get this strategy right, then the nature of the channel will shift from being driven by HR to being led by the employees themselves. At which point, the small fun incentives such as Starbucks Gift Cards become fun, additional benefits as part of the informal recognition that naturally occurs within the company.

The formal recognition programmes from the organisation should then become the icing on the cake. As we have discussed, most recognition programmes fail because they are not seen as being authentic because recognition is rarely part of the real culture. However, by ensuring managers are doing their part to recognise their people in real time, or as close to real time as possible, combined with an informal employee-led recognition culture, this sets a platform for official recognition programmes to be seen as a value add rather than a substitute for a lack of authentic recognition. The official programmes should be arranged at regular intervals and aimed at recognising different levels of accomplishment. This could mean you arrange 4 recognition programmes, one aimed at recognising something on a weekly basis, one on a monthly basis, one quarterly, and one annually. In a sales environment, this might be something as simple as sending an email to the whole department or company to recognise those who won new accounts on a weekly basis. Then on a monthly basis, all of the sales staff that beat target for the month get taken out for a fancy lunch. On a quarterly basis, you could arrange for some sort of offsite day trip for those who had consistently beaten target. Then on an annual basis, you could take the top salespeople away for a week of paid holiday.

The trick to making a recognition programme successful, though, is that it must be contextual to the organisation and team. This is why in addition to creating a programme that operates on a weekly, monthly, quarterly and/or annual basis, it is also wise to further separate this into recognition programmes that cover the whole company and those that focus on a single department. Otherwise, the programme that focuses on sales numbers is going to end up causing your operational staff to become demotivated and disengaged. After all, they are never going to be able to win formal recognition if the programme is only aimed at those who hit sales targets. So, a complimentary programme could be set up for other teams that also inspire high performance and reward the right behaviours contextual to their own roles and departments. Therefore, if an accountant redesigns a process that means they can complete the monthly accounts two days quicker, they could also qualify for the monthly achiever's lunch or get a shout-out via email. If they find a way to reduce your tax bill by a couple of percentage points to save the company money, that might be worth them getting a spot on the end-of-year trip. Perhaps the organisation could arrange a regular Oscar-style awards ceremony to take place after the quarterly town hall to recognise folks across each department. The possibilities are limited only by your own imagination.

Setting Standards

Recognition and praise are also a secret weapon in the arsenal of a manager and HR team. Do you want to know one of the fastest ways to create a high-performance culture within your team? Start praising and recognising the good things the people in your team are doing. Peer pressure often has negative connotations, but as an organisation, it is something you can use to drive positive outcomes within the company. When you start to consistently recognise and praise things a person is doing well, others in the company are going to start doing the same thing. This is because—except for some very enlightened monks and religious leaders—the vast majority of humanity craves acknowledgement and recognition. When you combine this with the competitiveness of the work environment and the desire for staff to progress in their career, you have a recipe for employees to push themselves to exceptional levels. The competitiveness and peer pressure will drive high performance in pursuit of recognition. If you congratulate Person A or Team A for beating Person B or Team B in sales last month, Person B or Team B are going to work twice as hard to ensure they do not lose the following month. At the same time, Person/Team A aren't going to want to lose their top spot. Also note that I have said praise Person A or Team A, and I did not say criticise Person B or Team B. That is a key difference. While fear can be a powerful short-term tool, it is not sustainable, which is why autocratic management styles don't produce long-term results. So, fear of criticism is not going to get you sustained results. However, if the teams are pursuing praise and recognition as opposed to trying to avoid criticism and punishment, that is sustainable over the long term. Everyone wants to be recognised.

There is a slippery slope to praise and recognition, though, and if used incorrectly, it can have disastrous effects on the company. This is because what you choose to praise sets the standards as to what employees should aspire to. If you are too stingy with the praise, employees will disengage because they are still not getting the recognition. But if you have taken anything from this chapter, you should understand now that you need to recognise the good as often as possible. However, the worst outcome is when you praise employees who don't deserve it. Just as being stingy can make the team feel unappreciated, if you praise them for even the smallest contribution, they will become entitled and complacent. While recognition can be one of the quickest ways to build a high-performance culture, recognition of those who don't deserve it can be one of the quickest ways to create a non-performance culture. If everybody gets a participation trophy or award regardless of their contribution, then the recognition is worthless. If it doesn't matter whether you finish first or last, then what is the point of trying to finish first?

There is often a mistaken belief that by recognising one person who did something exceptional, you will upset the others. But if you recognise that person and the others who have not done anything exceptional get upset—let them. It is much better than upsetting the high performer, who will then quit because you didn't recognise them. You set the standards for the team by what you choose to praise. If you praise an employee because they had 100% attendance, you are reinforcing the idea that just turning up to work is an achievement. If you recognise long service, you are reinforcing the idea that just keeping your job is an achievement. Your praise reinforces the standards for the company, and over time those standards become the expected norm. Once the team are consistently meeting those standards, you should then raise the bar to the next level. By doing this, not only are you consistently ensuring you have an engaged team because you are consistently recognising them, but at the same time, you are using your praise to drive performance higher and higher.

Finally, it is important to remember that all staff will have different personality types. This means that you need to be thoughtful about how you choose to recognise each individual in the company. If you have a top performer who is introverted and you choose to make them stand up in front of the entire company, collect an award and give a speech, that is not going to make them feel good. In fact, the same is likely to be true even within a small team meeting. In such a case, it would be better to recognise them privately without making a big deal out of it. If there needs to be some sort of companywide event, work around this. Having them record the speech on their phone in private and playing the recording at the event may be better than forcing them to stand up in front of the entire company and give a speech. Likewise, if you have an extrovert who likes to be the centre of attention, they may not value the recognition if it is quiet and discreet. The art of good management is to adapt your approach to get the best out of all employees—regardless of their personality or working style.

Chapter 5: Culture

While recognition is foundational to engagement, the culture of their team and wider organisation will also play a significant role in whether or not a member of staff remains engaged and motivated. Culture is often incorrectly considered a very 'fluffy' topic. Discussions of company culture can often lead to people wrongfully assuming they have to put pool tables and bean bag chairs in the office and have lots of fun. But let me be clear, a pool table or a bean bag chair does not equal engagement or culture. It simply means you have a bean bag chair or a pool table in the office. You can have pool tables, bean bag chairs, and free food in your office and still have a toxic environment. You could have nothing but desks and computers in the office and have an engaging environment. This is because, in reality, culture is about whether or not people fit into your environment and is not dependent on the office being cool and trendy.

The truth is that you could theoretically have a horrific micromanaging culture and high levels of engagement if every staff member came from the circa 17% of the population that can work in such an environment. The reason a micromanaging culture is generally toxic is because the majority of people simply cannot thrive in such an environment, but if you could theoretically only hire those who love micromanagement, everyone would be happy. They would not have to deal with all of those people who were criticising their style as they would all work in the same way. The business likely wouldn't achieve spectacular results, but in terms of engagement, you could theoretically keep the team well engaged in such a scenario. Of course, if you wanted to create a high-performance culture, then you would not want such an environment because as I have discussed in *The Manager Handbook*, autocratic styles will not drive a culture of high performance. But culture remains essential, and this is why research from Deloitte has shown that 88% of employees and 94% of business leaders consider a distinct culture important to a business's success. Further research has shown that businesses that are ranked among 'The Best Places to Work' in various awards consistently outperform their peers—both in terms of bottom-line profitability and stock market performance. As an organisation, the culture you create within the company will go a long way to defining how successful you are as a business. Culture, much like employee engagement and experience, is a business essential if you want to run a successful business. It is not a fluffy subject that is merely a nice to have.

Values

Most organisations struggle with culture change because culture and values are built over time. This is why in most organisations the words on a company website about the organisational culture and values are just that—words. They often have very little in common with the on-the-ground reality. In fact, when running culture workshops, I have come across many leaders who make jokes about their own organisational values because they are so meaningless. However, it is possible to build a team and/or organisation that is wholly aligned to the stated culture and values, and those organisations and teams are the ones that significantly outperform the others. Sadly, this doesn't happen overnight, and therefore most organisations fail to build effective culture. They think that changing the words on the website, sending out an email, or showing a PowerPoint slide at a town hall saying that their organisational values are 'agile' or 'innovative' or 'empathetic' or whatever makes it true. It doesn't. Cultural change is hard. People are not going to magically start acting differently on Monday because the CEO shared a couple of PowerPoint slides.

To build a winning culture, you have to start from where your existing management and employees are. Before you start designing where you want your company to go, you must first understand where the company is. Only then can you begin to plot the journey to where the organisation needs to be. People can't go from 10% to 100% overnight. You have to first get the team from 10% to 20%, then focus on getting them to 30%, and so on. If you fail to do this, the company will begin to fall apart, and you are going to have a lot of employees choosing to go elsewhere. While some attrition might be necessary to get you to where you need to go, you don't want a lot of it in the short term as it is going to severely impact your ability to deliver results. This is what many organisations get wrong, especially if there is new leadership and they want to take the business in a new direction. If you walk into the office and tell everyone that white is now black, they are gone. But if you slowly mix some black paint in with the white, it will start to turn grey before eventually changing colour completely. So, before changing the culture, it is vital to audit what the current baseline is—both its strengths and weaknesses.

This need to baseline and assess where the organisation currently is provides the HR department with a great opportunity to lead the way and map out exactly where the organisation is. The truth is that most HR teams are already sitting on this information if they have the last few years of engagement results. For example, the organisation may want to build a culture around the value of looking after its people. A quick glance at employee engagement survey results is going to tell you whether or not the employee base feels that the organisation and management do so. Even better, the results will also show you which teams and departments do this well and which ones don't. This provides HR with a heat map of what to prioritise and where across the organisation. This then allows solutions to be identified and incorporated into both the management training that should be happening throughout the year plus specific culture programmes that should be set up to drive alignment to the values of the organisation. This same approach is building a view across the organisation as a whole and a heat map of departments and teams as well. Does the organisation have a value of innovation? Well, if you have questions in your engagement survey about whether or not staff have the opportunity to raise new ideas and suggestions and/or whether they are taken on board, you are going to find out pretty quickly how accurate your value of innovation is.

The reason that the desired culture of many businesses—and by this, I mean the words they stick on their website—is usually far from the day-to-day reality is because leaders are not aligned to the culture. The honest truth is that culture starts at the top. A team is almost always a reflection of the person leading it. The only exception to this is a new manager or leader taking over a team, but after 18 months in charge of a team, there can be no excuses; the team reflects their leadership. I have consulted a number of organisations around the world that want to know why their employees aren't aligned to the values. The answer is almost always because of the leadership within the organisation. Your organisation might have a value of being employee-centric and caring for its employees. But if 3 of your 8 leaders consistently fire 33% to 50% of their team each year, then the reality is that the values don't exist in those teams. It doesn't matter what the website says or what the CEO presents at the town hall—the values are not present in these teams. Likewise, if you have an organisational value of being innovative, yet 6 of the 8 leaders have worked in the same industry for over 20 years and insist that things cannot be done differently, then again, the values are just words on a website or a slide. The same problems will persist again and again. Your leaders need to embody the values. So, if you do not like what you are seeing from your employees, you first have to look at who is leading those employees. If organisational management are not role modelling the expected behaviours, then why would your people?

This is once again where the HR team need to intervene. Just as with recognition, when it comes to culture, the role of HR is to bridge the gap between what the organisation and its people need and what the management team has the capability to deliver. One of the most common pushbacks from managers who want to avoid accountability for culture, and employee engagement results as a whole, is to claim they aren't responsible for how their people behave. But the fact remains that how people behave within the workplace is defined by how their immediate manager chooses to conduct themselves. The decisions they make become the norms they enforce. They can choose to punish a staff member for making a mistake, or they can choose to coach the staff member to learn from the mistake and improve. They can choose to force an employee to work while sick, or they can choose to tell them to go home and have the team cover. They can choose whether to take the team out to lunch or organise a cake every time it's someone's birthday, or they can choose not to celebrate it. They can choose whether to phone a member of staff on the weekend to get a report, or they can choose to wait until Monday morning. They can choose not to make a big deal about staff making deadlines, or they can hold them accountable for ensuring their work is up to the required standards. They can choose to push the team to find more efficient and innovative ways to work, or they can allow the team to continue to work as they always have. These decisions and hundreds of others lead to the culture within their teams.

This is also why there is always a disparity within an organisation when looking at engagement results. There are always outliers, which is because in those teams, the leadership is different to the others. Most teams may not feel recognised, but there will be others that do. If you dig into why that is by speaking to folks in those teams, they will share stories of what their manager does. When you speak to the other teams, you will likely discover that their managers aren't doing those things. This provides a great opportunity to then have those leaders and managers who are doing things well be role models to the others. By recognising and praising their behaviour, you will lead others beginning to follow suit. Likewise, it will provide you with a template of what you can build into both your management capability training sessions throughout the year, along with the customised interventions for teams that need it to fix the issues at hand.

Psychological Safety

In the first chapter of my book, *The Manager Handbook*, I outlined a series of characteristics that make a good manager and, in turn, lead to teams being engaged and delivering high performance. I am not going to repeat all of those characteristics here. However, one cultural factor underpins all of those characteristics, which sets the platform for high engagement, experience, and performance. This key cultural factor in building a high engagement and high performing team is psychological safety. The easiest way to think about psychological safety is the belief that you won't be punished or humiliated for speaking up with ideas, questions, concerns, or mistakes. If you want to create a successful organisation, you must enable a psychologically safe environment. Ask yourself, do the employees feel safe to take risks and be vulnerable in front of each other? If not, then there will be very little innovation or problem-solving within your company. This is because people will only innovate or try new things where they know it's safe to fail. If someone is in a situation where failure is punished, and they can't make mistakes, they are not going to want to take a risk. So, if no one is going to take a risk, they are going to hide problems and avoid responsibility, which means your business is going to stagnate and eventually fail. A team must feel they have the trust and support of management and the organisation as a whole. Without this, it is extremely difficult to create both high performing and high engagement teams.

The way management and HR choose to respond to typical day-to-day scenarios will go a long way in determining whether or not you have created a psychologically safe environment for staff. Ask yourself, what are the instincts of management when someone shares some bad news that could cause serious issues? Do they look to find the problem and try and find ways to improve the information people have, the conditions they have, or find ways to help? Or do they try and shut the discussion down and hope no one finds out about it? Or do they even go one step further, look for someone to blame, and throw them under the bus? What would you do if you were working on a team where things were going wrong? Would you feel comfortable telling people things are going wrong, knowing that others will support you and help you to resolve the issues? Or would you be scared about telling others about the challenges because you are worried you might get disciplined or worse? Is your answer different in the scenario where management are involved and the one where you are a team member? Did you also know that by creating a psychologically safe environment, you can get completely different results with the exact same workforce? Individual capability is not as important as the working environment. There is a wonderful example of this involving the General Motors California car plant.

Tesla's famous Fremont Factory in California actually has a long legacy going back all the way to the 1980s—way before anyone had heard of Elon Musk. Back in the 1980s, it was a General Motors (GM) factory, and it was the worst-performing GM factory in the whole of North America. It produced the worst cars, had the worst employee engagement levels, and workplace issues such as taking drugs and gambling were common. It was such a bad working environment that staff would even deliberately sabotage cars. It should come as no surprise that GM eventually made the decision to shut the factory down. Around that same time, GM and Toyota were looking to form a joint partnership. GM wanted to learn how to build smaller cars more profitably, which is something Toyota had perfected, and they had also heard about the famous Toyota management and production systems and were keen to get a closer look. Toyota was also keen to set up a factory in North America because the US Government was becoming upset about the fact that Japan was producing more high quality and cheaper cars, which was leading to a loss of American car manufacturing jobs.

The two firms formally engaged in a joint partnership, and GM offered Toyota the opportunity to use their old factory in Fremont. What was more surprising was that GM's workers' union convinced Toyota's management team to hire all of the old workers for the new factory. These were the same workers with the worst results and engagement levels out of all GM factories in North America. They were the same workers actively sabotaging the cars they were producing. This didn't seem to bother the Toyota management team, who sent the workers to Toyota City in Nagoya, Japan, to learn how Toyota workers build cars. They were introduced to all of the management techniques and processes used by Toyota. They then returned to the Fremont Factory to begin building cars, and within a few months, they were building the highest quality cars of any GM plant in North America and as high quality as the Toyota cars being produced in Japan. These were the exact same workers who, only a short while before, were producing the worst results and now producing the best results. It was clear that the people were not the problem. It was the ways of working under the previous leadership that was the problem.

So, what was different between the GM factory and the Toyota factory, which were in the exact same building, with the exact same workforce? Let's assume your job is to bolt in a seat. In a GM factory, the car comes along, and you are trying to bolt in the seat, but there is a mistake, and you need to pull it out and put in a new bolt. But before you can make that change to fix the error, you run out of space, and the car moves on to the next station. What do you do? Well, in a GM factory, nothing. The car moves on and continues to be built, and when it gets to the end of the line, it is tagged as not fit to drive because of the error. It gets put into the scrap heap. At the GM Fremont Factory, this was a common occurrence, where there always seemed to be some sort of error with the car. It might be a seat, it might be a door, it might be the engine, but there was always something. What was different in the Toyota factory was that when the car comes along, and you are trying to bolt the seat, if you can't get it done by about two-thirds of the way through your section, there is a line on the floor that reminds you that you are running out of time. In this scenario, the worker would pull a cord that alerts their manager, and the manager would come over to help them resolve the problem. If they can't resolve the problem by the time the car gets to the end of the section, they pull the cord again, and it shuts down the entire production line. This allows for the manager and staff to take the time to not only fix the problem but also reflect on ways to improve the process, so the problem doesn't reoccur. So rather than simply fixing the problem and pushing ahead, the team would take a moment to step back and think that maybe they need to redesign the wrench to operate at a different angle, or they need to use different kinds of bolts or other alternate solutions. Then there is a team of people at Toyota who will help you do just that. They will come back with a new wrench so you can try it, and if it works better, then production can begin again. But production will only recommence once the problem is solved.

The fundamental belief is that the manager's job is to help the people who work for them, and the staff have control over their work and have the ability to change their work based on the changing conditions and circumstances. This enables staff and management to take pride in their work and find joy in their jobs, meaning they will make sure they are building a high-quality product instead of focusing on volume to hit arbitrary KPIs. This is critical to what's different about the Toyota production system and their management style and working culture. The lesson that can be learnt from the Fremont Factory under two different leadership teams and cultural working styles is that the way to change culture isn't to start by changing how people think but instead to focus on changing how they behave. This is why so many teams and organisations fail to successfully change their culture. GM tried to replicate these results by taking the methodology and applying it to their other factories in America—but it failed. The reason for this is when a member of staff pulled the cord at another factory, the manager would show up, and instead of helping them, they would shout at them and discipline them. They may have had the methodology right, but the conduct of management did not facilitate a culture conducive to high performance.

Aligning Rewards to Culture

The reason why management in GM's other factories yelled at and disciplined staff instead of helping them is simple. Within GM, managers were rewarded based on how many cars came off the production line, regardless of whether they worked or not. Whereas within Toyota, management were incentivised based on the number of quality cars that were produced. This is why most organisational transformations fail. Most managers and organisations focus on the methodology or the framework, but it is the system of incentives within the organisation that will drive behaviour. The way in which management are incentivised will drive their behaviours which will facilitate the working environment of staff. A sales leader who is incentivised to bring in new sales will focus on as much new business as possible, regardless of the quality of that business. Another sales leader who is incentivised on the quality of sales being measured by how many customers are repeat customers will drive a completely different type of behaviour. A new framework or methodology is doomed to fail if management's incentives and, in turn, staff's KPIs/OKRs are not aligned to the new approach. If your sales leader is only paid based on new sales, your issues with the quality of business and customer satisfaction will continue until the manager is incentivised based on the quality of sales as opposed to the number of sales. Likewise, if you are in management, unless your staff's performance reviews and bonuses are tied into the new behaviours, they are going to continue to behave as before, and the culture will remain the same. So, if you are wondering why your sales team don't seem to be changing their behaviours despite all of your initiatives to get them to focus on the quality of sales as opposed to the number of sales, it's probably because they are still being rewarded for the number of sales. The same is going to be true of any other profession as well. People's behaviour in the workplace is always going to be driven by what they are measured on. If you want to drive a culture change within your team, this is an important weapon in your arsenal.

In addition to tying people's core KPIs to the culture and values you are trying to drive, you also need to factor this into your organization's promotion decisions. Let's assume you are trying to drive a culture of collaboration, as you have decided that's an important trait of successful organisations. Who do you think you should promote in the following example? Employee A, the clear number one salesperson, who made twice as much money as anyone else but has a reputation for being rude and disrespectful to others. Or Employee B, the number 6 salesperson who also beat their sales targets but made 3 times less than the number one salesperson, but who consistently goes out of their way to help others? Pretty much every single organisation in the world makes the mistake of choosing Employee A when it is clearly the wrong choice. It is clear that not only would Employee A make a bad manager despite being a great individual salesperson, but the person is also clearly not aligned to the organisational values and culture. Employee A should not only be passed over for promotion but should probably be managed out of the organisation, as their behaviour is in direct conflict with the culture and values of the company. They would also not create an environment that was psychologically safe. Employee B, on the other hand, has not only been a success themselves, and may not have been number one, but they beat their sales targets and are clearly aligned to the culture and values of the organisation and demonstrate the right kind of behaviour you would want from a manager within the firm.

Remember, if you want a positive culture that enables employees to outperform, it needs to be a healthy environment. Without a healthy environment, you can't have healthy employees, and if you don't have healthy employees, then you don't have a healthy business. This should be obvious, but far too many organisations get this wrong. If your employees are not well physically, mentally, or emotionally, the culture is going to be affected. If you want a positive and supportive culture, but all of your employees are overworked and stressed, this is not going to result in a positive and supportive culture. People are going to be tired and cranky and likely interact accordingly. If you want your culture to be a culture of high performance and innovation, but managers blame employees for any mistakes, you are not going to have the desired culture. Employees won't risk trying something new for fear of being blamed and fired. By creating a positive environment where employees are healthy physically, mentally, and emotionally a positive culture will naturally follow. It is vital for HR to ensure those in management are equipped, trained, and supported to facilitate the right culture. This should be done via the management capability training, supplemental culture programmes aligned to creating the right behaviours among all staff, and alignment of rewards and promotions to the values of the organisation.

Listen to Your Employees

It is also important to listen to what your staff are telling you. If there are consistent attrition, engagement, or behavioural issues within a specific team or the organisation as a whole, it is highly likely that management are the root cause. And this is OK. As the people who are responsible for making the decisions, they are going to make bad ones during the course of their time in charge. What will define the future of the organisation is not whether or not the organisation makes mistakes; the organisation is going to make lots of mistakes; it is whether or not you learn from them. The good news is that you are going to receive plenty of feedback from your people. There will be exit interview feedback when people leave, there will be engagement survey feedback, and there will also be direct and indirect feedback from your staff on a day-to-day basis. You might not like what you are hearing, but if you consistently hear the same thing again and again from multiple sources, it's likely to be true. This gives the organisation two choices when confronted with this feedback; you can act like

GM or Toyota. You can double down and insist it's your way or the highway, or you can realise your job is to support and help the organisation to achieve their goals. The choice is yours, but as we've discussed in the chapter about the role of HR in this book, a passive HR team that merely manage processes and don't proactively design solutions are not providing value.

Remember that no relationship can survive if one party simply refuses to listen to the other. Can you imagine a relationship with a spouse where you constantly ask them to simply do something differently as it makes you unhappy, and they refuse to change? How long do you think that relationship would last? The same is true of your employees. You constantly have an opportunity to improve the culture within the company, but you have to be willing to listen. Unfortunately, very few organisations listen. This is why most employees feel the whole employee engagement survey process is pointless. They raise the same issues year after year, and their manager or organisation simply refuse to acknowledge there is a problem. This only leads to one outcome.

If you want to have a positive culture where employees feel valued and happy and perform well, then an employee must feel they are valued. Not listening to them is one of the easiest ways to show you do not value them. It is also important to understand that a bad culture is not defined purely by being a rude or abrasive culture. In fact, one of the most common reasons organisations lose their high performers is because the culture is too 'nice'. As such, they do not single out their star performers for special recognition because they don't want other members of the staff to feel bad. This consistently leads to the high performers leaving, as there is no benefit to delivering exceptional results. When most in management or HR think about having to listen to their people, they naturally assume the complaints will be that they are being too strict, but that is not always the case. Sometimes the problem is the exact opposite. But the only way you will know what you need to do to improve the culture is to listen to your people.

Purpose

While values contribute to the culture, they are not the only thing that contributes to the culture of the team and/or organisation. The values essentially outline the behaviours of the team and/or organisation, but in isolation, they are not wholly binding. This is because while we want to spend our time in an environment aligned to our values, it does not provide us with a purpose. Purpose is the reason why we choose to spend our time in that environment in the first place. It is why we choose to get up in the morning and head to work and why we choose to stay late and go above and beyond. It is great to be surrounded by others who share your values, but you also need to have a reason to spend time with them in the first place. This is the purpose.

An example I use in my book *The Manager Handbook* is of a janitor at NASA who met President JFK in 1962. The President asked him what he was doing, and he said, 'I am helping put a man on the moon'. It is one of the best examples of how everyone in an organisation contributes to a larger purpose regardless of their own position in the hierarchy. I am sure he liked the values of NASA, but the reason he didn't go elsewhere is because he also believed in the mission. He wanted to go to work in the morning because he wanted to play his part in a cause he believed in. This is what you want for your employees as well. It is consistently proven that a purpose combined with the right values is near the top of most staff's wish lists in an employer. They want to work in a positive environment and feel like what they do matters. However, it is also consistently highlighted in employee engagement research that most employees have no idea how the work they are doing correlates to something bigger. Most people think the reason they are doing what they do is simply because their boss asked them to. So, despite staff consistently asking for some version of passion, purpose, or meaningful work, very few organisations articulate this to their teams. So, if you want to deliver a great employee experience and reap the benefits, this must be addressed.

If you want a high performing organisation, you need to provide your people with purpose. But a mistake many make when discussing purpose is to fixate on one type of purpose—the purpose of the organisation. This is undoubtedly an important purpose and one that should get attention. But the truth is there are other kinds of purposes too. A mistake that many organisations make is to forget that people are people. Sure, an employee might be hugely attached to a mission of saving the environment and, therefore, happy to work for a charity that saves the rainforests. But if a family member of theirs has a medical emergency and they now have to find a way to pay for treatment, they wouldn't think twice about joining a mining company cutting down the rainforest if it will ensure their family member gets the medical treatment they need. The concept of purpose is broad, and while in an ideal world, everyone would join only because they care about the purpose of the organisation, life happens. And at varying stages, other purposes will take priority. To create an effective culture that is purpose-led, you need to learn to operate in the space where purpose meets pragmatism.

Whenever there is a poll on the most meaningful and purposeful careers, the same professions consistently appear. Doctors, nurses, and teachers all appear on the list. Yet these same professions struggle with a lack of manpower. Everyone admires these professions and considers them to be meaningful and purposeful, yet there are not enough people choosing to pursue them. This is because there is more than one type of purpose, and your job is to work out what is most important to your staff at any given time and then provide them with a purpose that resonates with them to get up in the morning and come back into the office. I am sure your shareholders are wonderful people. But if you think your employees get up in the morning thinking, '*Yay, what a great day to make money for our shareholders*', you are deluded. Most businesses make the mistake of tying their purpose to a business metric such as more profitability and success for the organisation. Sure, that is important to ensure the business survives and thrives, but unless you are offering your people serious equity and giving them a cut of the profits, it's an approach that consistently fails to rally staff as a suitable purpose. The good news is that there are three broad categories of purpose most staff will fall into and ways to link this to their work. These categories are professional achievement, personal fulfilment, and community contribution.

Professional Achievement

The group of staff who derive their purpose from professional achievement are what I often refer to as the workhorses of the organisation. This is because a lot of their identity, self-worth, and sense of purpose are often tied up in their job. The good news is that this means very little needs to be done from a purpose perspective other than consistently linking what they do to the organisation. This is the 'we are sending a man to the moon' scenario. They might be the janitor, but they are playing their part. Because they are so focused on professional success, they obviously come to work wanting to put their best foot forward. This naturally leads to them taking on a lot of extra work, and they will end up putting in a lot of extra hours. So, your biggest challenge is often not to demotivate them or derail that sense of purpose by having them feel overlooked or undervalued.

This type of staff is often also wrongfully identified by most organisations and managers as their high performers. While this may be true in the early stages of a person's career, it is rarely true as they progress up the ladder. Taking on too much and having to work late and on the weekends consistently is rarely the sign of a high performer over the long term. Remember that quantity is not the same as quality. At a junior level, while you are gaining exposure and needing to learn, extra hours are usually a good sign. But as someone gets into their 30s and beyond, if they are chained to the desk all the time, it's usually a sign they are struggling with their work. Unfortunately, many corporate cultures promote presenteeism over results which has further led to the misconception that these folks are the top performers. But if you have a 35-year-old accountant who is working until midnight most nights and it's not year-end, that should be a red flag as they aren't going to be working efficiently. A high performer is someone who can deliver exceptional results while putting in the same or less effort as everyone else. Someone who is putting in a lot more hours is a hard worker, and they will get stuff done because of the extra time and effort they put in, but they are rarely an outperformer.

With that said, every organisation will usually have one of these people in each team who is an invaluable team member. They may not be the superstar, but they are incredibly important and play their part in the team. To use a sporting analogy, not everyone can be Cristiano Ronaldo. He is widely regarded as one of the greatest footballers of all time. He is also arguably a legend for Manchester United, having won numerous trophies for them and played with some of the all-time greats. This same accolade would not be directed at John O'Shea. Yet John O'Shea played in the same team as Cristiano Ronaldo over 200 times. John O'Shea also won 2 more English Premier League Championships than Cristiano Ronaldo and was also his teammate when they won European and World Titles. John O'Shea is, of course, not on the same level as Cristiano Ronaldo, but every team need a workhorse who gives their all for the team and provide the platform for the superstars to win the game.

The difference between sport and the corporate world is that in the corporate world, John O'Shea would have been promoted over Cristiano Ronaldo because, on paper, he achieved more at Manchester United. He also played nearly 200 competitive games more for them. Cristiano Ronaldo won 9 trophies in his nearly

200 hundred games with the team. By contrast, John O'Shea won 14 trophies in nearly 400 games for Manchester United, but 9 of those came while he played in the same team as Ronaldo. The teams he played in only won 5 other trophies in circa 200 games without Cristiano Ronaldo. The key to providing purposes to those who focus on professional outcomes is to ensure you suitably recognise their contributions to the organisation's success. They will take on the extra projects and the extra hours to help the team, but because they also need to be provided with professional recognition, you need to be able to balance this. All teams need those dedicated team players who put in the hard work, and it's important to ensure their contribution is recognised. But it is also important to keep in mind that a John O'Shea isn't going to win you the game on their own. John O'Shea and Cristiano Ronaldo were given the same medals for being in the same team and winning the same competitions, but Cristiano Ronaldo was the one who also received the individual accolades. The challenge in the corporate world is that your own John O'Shea will feel they are the one who should be promoted because they played twice as many games as Ronaldo and won more trophies. Business Management isn't always easy, and this is one of those examples, as you won't be able to keep everyone happy forever.

Personal Fulfilment

To continue my example from the previous chapter, it would, of course, be disrespectful to Cristiano Ronaldo to imply he wasn't a workhorse. His work ethic is famous. But the difference with Cristiano Ronaldo is that he is much more than just a football player. This is a common trait among many high performers. You see, high performers are rarely a high performer in only one area of their lives. They apply this same approach to all aspects of their lives. In fact, some research by Brendan Bouchard found that a large number of high performing corporate professionals have similar energy levels to professional athletes. It is quite common for a high performer to also be a triathlete, a marathon runner, a musician who plays in a band as well, or something else. This is why high performers are unlikely to be in the professional achievement category. They expect, want, and will earn professional recognition, but they often have a lot more going on in their lives than just their job. They might take on an extra project, but they aren't staying at the office until midnight every night to get it completed. They are getting it completed by 6 pm, and they are then going to train for the marathon or play a gig or whatever. This is why they are a high performer.

Cristiano Ronaldo may be one of the greatest footballers ever, but he is not just a footballer. He also owns several businesses ranging from clothing and retail businesses to hotels, fitness centres, and restaurants. He even owns a private jet rental business! He is also a dedicated father and has five children, and he still finds the time to do philanthropic work. There are two mistakes most organisations and managers make when dealing with such people. The first is to make a judgement that they are not dedicated because they have the audacity to have priorities other than work. This is usually the result of toxic cultures that can exist if you end up promoting your professional achievement folks into your leadership ranks as opposed to your true high performers. Again, I will repeat that quantity is not the same as quality. The second mistake is to try and force them to choose between work and their other priorities. This is a deal breaker for these types of individuals, and it will cost you a high performer. If you tell your team member they will need to stop running outside of work hours because you want them to spend their personal time working, that is just terrible management. If the member of staff falls in this category of personal fulfilment, it means they are a true high performer doing good work both in and out of the office. This means there are no issues with their performance, so what they are doing outside of work makes no difference.

Instead, you should try to combine their passions to lock in these high performers for the long term to your team or organisation. This means they are able to derive their full purpose while being part of your team. For example, if you have someone who competes in marathons, ask them if they would like to set up a fitness community within the organisation. Perhaps they could set up a running club, meaning that either before or after work or maybe even during lunchtime, a group of staff will all go out for a run together. It will allow them to work on their other key goals while being part of the organisation and, at the same time, create a sense of community and belonging within the organisation. This will align their purpose both inside and outside of the office and create a positive culture simultaneously. Likewise, if someone plays in a band, ask if they would like to get a musical group together in the office. Maybe they could play at company events, or maybe it's as simple as organising a monthly karaoke team night out. This allows your high performers to contribute to their purpose within your organisation while also allowing it to extend beyond the organisation. It also allows you to get the best of both worlds. You keep a high performing superstar while also keeping them highly engaged and allowing a positive culture to be built throughout the organisation as people see that they aren't treated as just mindless drones who are not allowed to have lives beyond the office.

Community Contribution

The final group of employees fall under a category of purpose that I call community contribution. The vast majority of the workforce falls into this category. These are the people who aren't desperately trying to get recognition from the workplace by working all hours or trying to climb mountains, run marathons, and have side hustles on top of their job. They want to enjoy their work and do their best, but they simply have other priorities in life. To them, work is simply a job, promotions and pay rises are great, but honestly, they aren't going to kill themselves to get it. As long as they can pay their bills and pursue their interests, they are happy. The surprising truth is also that your team and organisation need people like this. While most management and HR experts will tell you that you need to make all of your staff live and die by the organisational purpose and strategy, you really don't. The majority in a large organisation, even those who are seen as purpose-driven, never achieve this. If this was the norm, then nobody would be watching the new show on Netflix or checking out that cool restaurant after work.

If everyone is trying to work all of the hours available and has no other priority but to work or deliver outstanding results, you are also going to create a horrible toxic culture where everyone is competing with everyone else—and they will screw each other over to win. It is impossible for you to promote and recognise the whole team, so if you have an entire team of driven people, it will descend into a political nightmare when you recognise a few but not all of them. The reality is that you only need about 1/3 of your team or workforce to be made up of those driven by professional purpose or personal fulfilment. Most teams and organisations struggle with any more than this unless they are a start-up, as the nature of start-ups is that it's a group of highly driven people trying to start something new. But as they scale, it's impossible to maintain being a majority driven by professional purpose or personal achievement.

This group of staff are also the ones that most managers and organisations struggle to provide a purpose to. How do you align folks to a purpose when they aren't entirely focused on high levels of achievement? But this is often a fallacy. Most people will have some sort of purpose or priority. It is just that management and organisations often fail to think beyond a person's job. Every single person on this planet has priorities, and the trick to delivering outstanding results within your team is to link their priorities to the organisation. This is actually where your organisational culture and sense of community truly have a chance to shine. If you get it right, you will have a culture everyone wants to be part of; if you get it wrong, then your team or organisation is just the same as all the others who don't care about its people beyond them delivering the required results.

Your people will have families; they will have hobbies, and they will have causes they are passionate about—all beyond whatever their job title says. So, if you have a group of people with family as a number one priority, then encourage this group of people to set up a community within the organisation for parents. They could share tips and advice on balancing work with parental responsibility; they could arrange play dates, share day care, arrange social events for staff that are child friendly, and so on. You could have members of staff enjoying playing some kind of sport. Encourage them to set up a team or group in the office who can play together or train together. You will have folks who enjoy certain types of music, food, travel, languages, or books. There will be those who are passionate about causes such as climate change, helping the homeless, taking care of the elderly, or raising money for cancer research. Encourage all of your people to bring their full selves to work and allow them to build meaningful connections with their peers who share those same interests. It will allow them to connect their purposes with working for your team or organisation and building a strong employee-led culture.

The strongest and most successful cultures are those that are organic and employee-led. A reason most organisations fail to develop a strong culture is because they try to drive culture from the top down. They will say here are the 5 things we care about as an organisation, and these are the 5 things we will all do. Theoretically, it makes sense, and it looks great on a set of PowerPoint slides. But the world is a wonderfully diverse place, and your people aren't all going to care about the same 5 things with the same level of strength. It would be autocratic to think otherwise. Instead, you are going to end up with some people who are passionate about one topic, others who are passionate about 8 different things, and they all want to get involved or show their interest in such things in different ways. Let them!

This is how you build an authentic culture that resonates with your people because the culture truly reflects who your people are. This also promotes true inclusion and diversity because they can bring their full authentic self to work and share it with others. If a group of your staff love the marvel movies, encouraging them to get together to watch the movies after work once a month is a great idea. You may think this doesn't have anything to do with work. Still, the fact that they will be spending time building connections with each other about something—even non-work-related—will lead to a better team environment and a more collaborative culture. This is an obvious and basic concept that, unfortunately, most organisations and managers fail to grasp. But if you are able to unify your team not just around a professional purpose but a broader alignment around other shared interests and priorities, you will build a strong, authentic culture that allows your team to outperform expectations.

Team Building

Building an effective culture, of course, goes beyond providing a purpose and outlining a set of values. In order to mould all of this together to get the desired outputs, you have to also get your employees working as a team. A team of average capability will always outperform a highly talented group of individuals. You will likely have heard phrases such as 'teamwork makes the dream work' or 'if you want to go fast, go alone; if you want to go far, go together'. These phrases and many others like them are both well known and speak a universal truth. If you want to achieve something big, you require a team working together in order to achieve it. If we revert to our example of the janitor at NASA, you might have the best astronauts and rocket engineers in the world, but they aren't going to be nearly as productive without the janitors. Everyone within a team plays their part. For every Cristiano Ronaldo, you need a John O'Shea. Your role is to help turn them from a group of individuals that work together into a cohesive unit complementing each other's strengths and mitigating each other's weaknesses. Team bonding is a critical component in being able to achieve this. Quite simply, if a person in your company needs help from their team member (who is also likely to be incredibly busy), the chances of that team member helping will often depend on whether or not they like that person. Now, while it's impossible to get everyone to be best friends, depending on how effective you are at building culture within the organisation, you can make it more likely that they will help out. The best cultures and environments are ones where they don't help out because the boss tells them to. They help out because they genuinely want to help a teammate even if they themselves are busy.

The best way to build this rapport among the team is with some good old-fashioned team bonding activities. Now, when I speak about team bonding exercises, I don't mean those corporate team building exercises that we all roll our eyes at and despise. I am not telling you to run out and sign your employees up to do loads of trust falls and other sorts of exercises. While there are benefits to doing some of those traditional corporate things, the truth is that most staff (and management) can't stand them, and they can often be counterproductive. It is another equivalent of having organised fun, and organised fun is not fun. Team building, just like fun and recognition, should be more authentic. You are much more likely to build an effective culture by ensuring the managers take the teams out for lunch once a month and banning all work topics as conversation than doing trust falls or other corporate team bonding activities. The reason for this is simple. For people to build authentic relationships, they need to engage in authentic conversations with each other. While you can't force them to build relationships with each other, you can make it more likely that they will build these relationships. A simple way to do this is by providing opportunities for the team to get to know each other beyond their jobs. The easiest way to do this is with social events that do not require a huge time commitment.

Take the teams out to lunch on the last Friday of each month (or whatever day is convenient), ensure that you celebrate everyone's birthday with some sort of lunch, or have everyone sign a card. Play secret Santa at Christmas, and organise an after-work drink or meal to celebrate people achieving some sort of professional or personal milestone. It honestly isn't that hard to do. Likewise, set up WhatsApp groups, Slack channels, or something relevant and encourage the team to share non-work-related activities such as photos of their kids' school play, their dog playing fetch, their latest holiday photos, or whatever. Your role is to provide the platform allowing everyone else to get to know each other better. If your teams are working remotely, you can set up virtual lunches and other sessions. It doesn't need to be overly complex, and you are only limited by your imagination. The stronger the relationships within the teams, the better your organisation will perform. Once you have laid the foundations with these basic activities, it is more likely that a formal team bonding exercise such as an escape room or a scavenger hunt will deliver the desired results.

One of the biggest changes you will see in your employees as they begin to bond is around their communication with one another. This is because no company can function effectively without communication, and the better employees communicate, the better the results will be. The reason most team building activities fail is because you can't send employees away for a half-day session to learn team communication frameworks or methodologies and then expect them to just start communicating differently with one another. Academically it may make sense to teach a 'communication framework', but the truth is that humans don't work that way. But if your employees become more social with one another and feel like they know each other, they will naturally communicate more with one another. This means the employees are more likely to be open with each other about challenges they are facing and, therefore, more likely to receive help. Likewise, it means the employees are less likely to shy away from difficult conversations. It is quite common in the corporate world that people are afraid to have difficult conversations. If someone needs to provide some constructive feedback, they often worry about any potential negative reactions. But, if your employees have a strong rapport, it becomes a lot easier to share that someone made a mistake or that some kind of behaviour is inappropriate. The best companies are those that communicate openly and candidly without fear.

This brings us to another huge benefit of effective team building—trust. If you want an effective organisation that can work together and outperform, employees need to be able to trust each other. Quite simply, if there is a lack of trust, there will be a lack of sharing. If someone needs help but feels like their colleague will throw them under the bus, they are unlikely to reach out for help. But if they know they can rely on their colleague to help them out, they will ask for help. This element of trust is critical for a company to function properly. If one employee knows they are bad at a certain thing and another colleague is better, they are much more likely to collaborate and get the best result if they trust each other. This also means the organisation is significantly more productive as employees will share the workload and utilise each other's strengths accordingly.

But as a species, we are all filled with bias, and in most corporate workplaces filled with politics and fear, trust is not something easy to come by. At the most basic level, though, familiarity breeds trust. The more you feel you know someone, the more likely you are to trust them. Think about this logically. If there was an emergency and you had to leave your child with someone for an hour, given a choice, who would you leave them with? Person A—who is a complete stranger you do not know, or Person B—who is someone from work you interact with a few times a week? It is, of course, Person B. Now, would you rather leave them with someone from work you kind of know or a close family member? It is, of course, a close family member. So, while you can't force employees to trust each other, by providing the platform for them to become more familiar with each other— by getting to know each other as more than just the role they perform in the office—you will make it more likely that your employees have higher levels of trust than other organisations. This should translate into better performance as well.

There is also a reason sport is usually at the forefront of social issues, and this is because it naturally breaks down barriers. One thing you learn early on when playing sport is that the only thing that matters is that the team win. It doesn't matter if you score 5 goals every game if the team lose every week. But what is also prevalent in such an environment is that you do not care what background your teammates are from. All that matters is that you all play your part to help the team win. It does not matter if the team members are from different genders, races, religions, sexual orientations, or any other kind of difference. Everyone is included and works together to achieve the same goal. It's why in the Israeli football league, you will find Israelis and Palestinians playing on the same side. It's why when you look at any top-level sports team, there are incredible examples of diversity and inclusion all around. When the whistle blows, people are not whatever background they are part of, but instead a member of the team. Team bonding allows for a similar opportunity for barriers to be broken down within your own organisation.

Bias is a real thing; it has been proven time and time again we are more likely to side with those to whom we can relate. But this bias extends beyond obvious things such as race or nationality. An example I shared in my first book, *The Employee Handbook,* discussed a study that showed people were more or less likely to help someone depending on the sports jersey someone wore. So, if person A were injured and were wearing a Manchester United sports jersey, Person B would be more or less likely to help them if they were or were not also a Manchester United fan. So, a white Manchester United fan would be more likely to help a Black or Asian Manchester United fan than a white Liverpool fan, for example. So, by ensuring your employees bond and feel like one team, you are much more likely to have an inclusive organisation than those who do not feel like one team. This is also a reason why most inclusion and diversity efforts fail within organisations. They often focus on the token diversity element— e.g., the race, sexual orientation, or gender of individuals— without remembering it is the inclusion part allowing for everyone to feel part of the same team that delivers the results. If you are able to get a diverse team working together, you will reap the benefits because, as we have discussed elsewhere in this book, diverse teams consistently outperform others.

Inclusion & Diversity

Inclusion and diversity are business essentials, just as employee engagement and culture are. The reason is simple. Businesses that have a more diverse workforce at all levels make more money than businesses that do not. This is because the more people you have with different ideas, views, and perspectives, the stronger your business will be. Rather than only being able to approach things from one angle, your organisation will be able to take the best of multiple perspectives and create something significantly stronger. This messaging often gets missed when communicating inclusion and diversity programmes. They are often positioned as fluffy, nice to have ideals as opposed to business essentials to deliver outstanding results. Due to this lack of clarity in communication, many organisations fail to see a return on their investment into inclusion and diversity. This is because failure to understand how inclusion and diversity benefit an organisation often leads to a focus on diversity rather than inclusion. But let's be clear, without inclusion, there can be no diversity.

One of the easiest ways to grasp the difference between inclusion and diversity is to imagine a group of guests at a dinner party. Let's assume you have invited your team over for dinner one evening. Your colleagues are a wonderfully diverse group of people. One of your colleagues eats absolutely everything, another doesn't eat pork, and another dislikes beef. In addition to those 3 colleagues, your other colleagues consist of a vegan, a vegetarian, and someone who is allergic to peanuts. What do you serve for dinner? Your guests are diverse, but if you insist on serving steak with a peanut sauce because that's your favourite, then how many of the guests are going to eat the meal? This is the difference between diversity and inclusion. Your organisation might have ticked the box and hired lots of people that are different, but to build a winning culture, you need to also ensure they all feel included. Otherwise, you are merely taking a check-the-box approach to inclusion and diversity, and if you do that— how many of them do you think are coming over for dinner next time? If they were not included in the meal, then the invite was meaningless.

At the same time, if you asked that group of diverse individuals to come up with an ideal meal, they might just have come up with an innovative new product. Imagine a plant-based steak that looked and tasted like beef but could be eaten by everyone? Well, that product now exists, and Impossible Foods, one of the leaders in that space, was valued at $7 billion at the time of writing. This is how a diverse group can benefit an organisation when brought together to work in partnership. By bringing together each individual's different needs, wants, experiences, and perspectives, your company is able to create something new that can drive better outcomes for your customers. But in order to reap the benefits of inclusion and diversity, your organisation has to be able to enable a culture that supports inclusion and diversity.

The starting point to enabling this culture and a successful inclusion and diversity strategy begins with the managers within the organisation. Just as with culture as a whole and the overall employee engagement and employee experience (and, for that matter, any other project, programme, or objective), it will succeed or fail based on the actions of management. As I have said elsewhere in this book, you can have the best policies and processes in the world, but if your management group do not abide by them, then everything will fall apart. You could have the most forward-thinking inclusion and diversity policies in the world, but if your managers don't enforce them, then it does not matter. This is often where the programme will fall down. I have seen this play out numerous times.

For example, I will always remember one organisation that implemented equal paternity leave and maternity leave policies. The logic was that if a man or woman was going to take the same time off when they had a child, there was very little reason to discriminate against hiring women. Despite the policy, numerous managers in the organisation still refused to hire women because they believed they would have family commitments and the men would not. The organisation also failed to act against those managers who were discriminating against women. They were not hiding the discrimination; they were openly stating they would not hire women. So, the programme failed, and the organisation failed to get more women into the organisation. What is worse, this organisation actually won several inclusion and diversity awards for having the policy despite the fact that it was a complete failure. It is, therefore, vital that the organisation inclusion and diversity programmes and policies are also built into the management capability programmes the organisation put in place. Without this, the programmes will never take hold in the company.

With management being educated and on board with the inclusion and diversity agenda, the next step for the organisation is to re-assess its policies with a lens of not just diversity but inclusion also. It is important to remember that diversity is incredibly easy to achieve. For example, if an organisation wanted to hire a number of women or individuals from specific ethnic minorities or other groups, it is very straightforward. There are literally thousands of community-specific organisations around the world to partner with to help drive diverse hiring strategies. However, as we have already discussed, it is one thing to invite people from these groups to dinner and another thing entirely to ensure the meal is also something they can eat.

A simple example of this could relate to cultural holidays. In western culture, Christmas is a public holiday, so everyone gets the day off. However, in Japan, Christmas is a normal working day. Therefore, if a westerner is working in Japan, they need to use their annual leave entitlement to take Christmas day off. The same is true of minority groups in western culture. A couple of billion people celebrate Chinese New Year and Diwali worldwide, yet people from these groups would need to use their annual leave entitlement to celebrate a cultural holiday. Therefore, an inclusive programme could be to allow individuals a couple of extra days off a year related to relevant cultural holidays. It is, therefore, important that HR review all existing policies and ensure they are aimed at being as inclusive as possible. For example, an organisation may provide some flexibility to parents with young children as they may need to work from home when a child is sick. But what about a single person who has no kids but needs to look after a sick relative? The list of possibilities to enhance HR policies to be more inclusive is practically endless, and it is a great way for HR to lead from the front and drive a more inclusive culture with items that fall under their direct responsibility. Although, as discussed, it is vital this is done in conjunction with ensuring management abide by such initiatives, or they become meaningless.

In addition to ensuring HR policies are consistently reviewed and rewritten to be more inclusive of all staff, there also needs to be a sustained communication strategy throughout the organisation. This is because there are very few individuals who are openly discriminatory. Conscious bias exists—and it would be foolish to claim otherwise—but it is something that only a small percentage of a population exhibits. The truth is that most bias within an organisation is unconscious. In fact, one of the biggest pushbacks against the so-called 'woke' culture currently is because people feel they are unfairly tagged as being racist, sexist, or so on, simply for not fully understanding how their words could be misconstrued. The truth is that ignorance of another group's challenges is a bigger barrier to achieving equality and an organisation's need for an inclusive and diverse environment as opposed to hate for that same group. Fortunately, ignorance can be improved by communication and education, and again, HR are in a position to directly influence this discussion within a company.

It takes very little effort to create some sort of weekly newsletter, highlighting issues and sharing stories to help employees learn more about each other's cultures and backgrounds. This can help people understand how they may use a microaggression against another group without even realising it. A microaggression is an unintentional action that discriminates against a minority group. This newsletter (and it doesn't just have to be a newsletter, there could be videos, segments at weekly management meetings, etc., you are only limited by your imagination and capacity) could cover topics such as how arranging team drinks after work could create an uncomfortable environment for certain groups and provide other suggestions for more inclusive team get-togethers among numerous others.

On top of this, one of the easiest ways to show employees that you respect their culture and traditions is to also celebrate events at work. If you have an Indian member of staff, arrange a team lunch or dinner to celebrate Diwali. If you have someone who is Chinese, make sure you do something for Chinese New Year. The same goes for International Women's Day, Black History Month, and a whole host of other dates that can be put on the calendar. It also costs nothing to send an email around to the organisation to highlight each cultural event and tradition so that people are aware of why their Thai colleagues have taken the week off in April to celebrate their new year with water fights or why the 4th of July is important to a company's American employees or the 25th of April to Australian employees, etc. HR should have data on the demographics of those within the organisation, so it should be relatively straightforward to build out a year-round calendar. This can then be combined with the employee-led community groups that exist within the organisation, such as the Bhangra Dance Group or Women in Tech, etc., that should be empowered to run employee-led initiatives all year round.

As you go through the process of building out your inclusion and diversity programmes, it is important to continue to bring the focus back to why diversity and inclusion are important. Study after study proves that a diverse workforce results in better business results than workforces that are not diverse. The reason for this is simple, the more people you have from different backgrounds with different ideas, the better the end product will be. Different perspectives will see problems or solutions that someone else may not. I know I have repeated this several times now, but it is important this is remembered. Otherwise, the programmes and agenda will slip back into being seen as a nice to have as opposed to the business essential topic that it is. If your organisation wants to be successful, then the more differing viewpoints and perspectives, the better. I have outlined under the diversity in leadership section of this book how benchmarks can be used to ensure your organisation is on the right track. By using the community that your organisation (or office if you are a large organisation with multiple locations) is part of. In addition to this, an additional lens to further enhance the benchmarks would be to ensure your workforce mirrors the demographics of the market they operate in.

One of the best examples of this in action is the success of Sara Blakely's business Spanx. She has built a billion-dollar business that disrupted the traditional pantyhose business. After growing frustrated with other products in the industry, she set out to create her own product. As she began to embark on developing a better product to alleviate the discomfort suffered by her and many other women all around the world, she stumbled onto the root cause of the problem. As she began talking to manufacturers, she realised she had not encountered any women. Then the issue dawned on her, as she has outlined several times in interviews as follows:

I kept talking to all these men, in the process of trying to make my product, and I remember thinking, "Where are the women? Why am I not speaking to any women here?" And then it dawned on me that maybe that's why our pantyhose had been so uncomfortable for so long because the people making them aren't wearing them, and if they are, they're not admitting it, [laughter] so, nobody really wanted to go there. And I learned that when you're making . . . When the industry was making the product, that they took the same size waistband and put it on every pair. So, a size small woman and a size extra-large woman was getting the same waistband, so that they could cut costs during production. And I also learned that they were putting a tiny rubber cord inside of our waistbands. Well, I immediately said, "Guys, this is not working. We have been miserable, we can't breathe, we're cutting our waistbands. A small woman wants a small waistband and a large woman wants a large waistband, it makes sense." So, with Spanx, all of the waistbands were sized accordingly and that was the first change I made.

Just as with the example of the dinner party, this is a clear example of why it is important for a business to have diversity within the organisation. Sara Blakely's desire for a better product was not unique. It was a common problem for most of the customers of pantyhose. But there was no one in the organisations making the product who could provide this voice. As a result, those businesses have lost out on hundreds of millions of dollars in revenue. The same is true for other businesses around the world each and every day. This is why it is vital to have a workforce that is representative of the customers and communities that it serves and supports.

Chapter 6: Employee Development

The desire to progress and develop is an essential human need. As I outline in my book *The Manager Handbook,* this is best explained by Maslow's Hierarchy of Needs. Without going into a long explanation of the hierarchy and psychological theory, it essentially says that humans have 5 different levels of needs. This starts with the most basic needs, such as food and water, through to the ultimate goal, which according to this theory, is to reach the fifth level of the hierarchy, which is essential to fulfil your potential and achieving all you could possibly achieve. But the only way to progress from one level to another is to fully satisfy your need at the previous level. For example, if you can't fulfil the basic need of having enough to eat, it's highly unlikely you are going to be focused on trying to become an expert in your field. But once you meet your needs at a certain level, then the attention always turns to what is next. Our entire civilisation is essentially built on the story of human progress and development. The same innate desire will exist in some shape or form in all of your employees.

Don't believe me? How many employees do you know that don't want to be promoted, don't want to earn more money, don't want to have a comfortable retirement, don't want to be able to send their kids to a nicer school, or provide their family with a better house, or to ensure they are able to look after their parents in old age and all of the other desires we have for our loved ones? Not many, right? Now, how would someone provide themselves and their family with all of these things? Well, they would need to earn more money. How do they make more money? Well, they have to progress and grow their careers. So, why would someone want to stay working for an organisation where there were limited opportunities to grow and develop? Quite simply, they would not. This is something consistently backed up by research as well. Research has shown that 82% of staff would quit their jobs if they lacked career progression opportunities. A further study by LinkedIn showed that 93% of employees would stay with a company longer if that employer invested in their careers and provided them with growth opportunities. A further study found that career development boosts employee engagement more than purely providing staff with learning and development opportunities. There are many other studies all saying similar things as well.

Unfortunately, despite employees consistently telling organisations what they would like from them, these words often go unheard. Businesses have long understood the negative impacts of attrition. Employee attrition has always been costly for companies, and this should not be new information to anybody. But what is fascinating is that the problem is getting worse, and organisations are still failing to adapt. Further research from Gartner showed that since the financial crisis of 2008, many organisations went through streamlining exercises that dramatically removed several layers of middle management in order to reduce costs. But the knock-on effect on staff over the next decade was significant. Today's average employee actually spends 50% longer in the same role than before 2008 due to the reduction in promotion opportunities caused by a cull in the ranks of middle management.

Professional Development

When the topic of professional development for employees comes up, there is almost always a dilemma within organisations. They understand its importance, but they will rush to explain how it is impossible to provide career development to all of the team. They will explain how it is impossible to promote all of the team every year. After all, you can't just provide constant growth opportunities, right? Actually, you can. At the core of the confusion is that many conflate professional development and promotions. The truth is that you can continue to grow your people every year without needing to promote them every year. There will, of course, be a couple of high performers who are just amazing and who may actually deserve a promotion every year—it's rare, but these people do exist, and your company should reward them. But the truth is that the majority of staff are by definition average and, as such, would be satisfied with career development at an average pace.

But let's be clear, professional development is not purely about a promotion. Professional development is about ensuring your people are developing. This can be done easily without needing to link it to a promotion every single time. A promotion may be part of someone's professional development journey at some point, but it is not the only purpose of professional development. Someone needing to learn how to code a new software and their desire to become CTO one day is part of a spectrum. They can

149

learn how to code a new software over the next 6 months, but their ambition to become CTO one day is a very long-term objective. The person is not going to quit if they aren't promoted to CTO this year if they are currently 6 career levels below CTO. They are also not going to expect to be promoted 6 times in 6 years to become CTO. Pretty much all of your employees are reasonable people who understand that such a journey might take 20 years.

The real problem your organisation needs to address is that very few companies actually plan for their employees' career development long term. Career development is often seen as a happy accident. An opportunity may arise for a training course, or there is a year-end quota to fill for promotions, and so their manager reacts. Or someone resigns, and the manager can't find a good external candidate, and so they provide an opportunity to one of the existing team to step up. But the number of managers or HR teams who can tell you what their plans for their people are for the next 3 years is incredibly rare. This needs to be addressed to ensure employee engagement and experience remain strong over the long term. An employee might have some great goals and like the culture and their colleagues, but if they aren't going to grow professionally, then they will still leave. It is, therefore, imperative that an organisation ensure that every employee has at least a three-year development plan in place. The reason the plan should last for 3 years is because this is the typical tenure of an employee in a role. In the first year, they are learning their new role, in year two, they are excelling and improving, and in year three, they begin to wonder what is next. So, if there is nothing on the horizon for them with their current organisation, then they are going to look elsewhere. This is essentially why the average tenure of most employees is around 3–4 years with an organisation. They get into year three and begin to realise there is no growth, and so they decide to go elsewhere.

The aim of the organisation's professional development programme should be to shift the approach from a reactive career development strategy to a proactive strategy. This means that rather than career development being opportunistic based on something happening, career development is instead planned for and expected across the whole organisation. This will lock your people into the organisation for the long term providing a great employee experience and significantly higher levels of engagement. However, when designing the programme, it is important to remember that just as professional development and promotions are not the same thing, the same is true of training. As part of one's professional development, a person may undergo some training, but training on its own is not professional development. Training is something a person receives to fill in a knowledge or skill gap to make someone more effective. Professional development is a long-term plan that factors in both an employee's and the organisation's growth over the longer term.

As part of a career development plan, there may be training, coaching, mentoring, additional projects, promotions, and so on. But any of these in isolation are not career development. For example, sending a member of staff on a design thinking course but then not providing them with opportunities to put those new skills into action means you have not provided the person with a development opportunity. You just sent them away to get a certificate for something they are unable to use. In fact, by doing this, you are making it more likely that the person quits so they can put the skills to use elsewhere as they want to develop. So, to ensure longevity, there must be a focus on an employee's career path over the long term. It should come as no surprise that organisations that offer their employees jobs as opposed to careers see significantly higher employee turnover. If someone is performing a job, they will happily do the job elsewhere for more money. If someone is building a career and they have clear goals and a good environment, they are going to stick around.

There is also an important nuance to ensuring your professional development programme is a success. The type of development must be tailored specifically to each individual based on their own wants and desires. Neither the organisation nor the employee benefit by forcing mandatory development in an area the employee doesn't want. It is one of the worst things you can do. This is because everyone has a different set of ambitions for their own careers. This means that career development for one person may be to climb the ladder and move into management, but for another, they may not want more responsibility, and for their development, they just want to develop their technical skills and become better at their current role. In both scenarios, this is professional development. But if you push the person who doesn't want to move into management into a supervisor role, then they are going to quit. Another common mistake is to promote someone on paper, but in reality, they are still doing the same job. So, calling someone who was an 'analyst' a 'senior analyst' doesn't mean they were promoted if they see their day-to-day duties as being precisely the same. If they do not feel they are doing new things and growing, then they are still going to quit because you have not really promoted them. All you have done is changed their job title, but in reality, they are still doing the same thing, and so they have not had any professional development.

The starting point of building a professional development programme for each member of staff has to begin with the manager and HR sitting down with each employee and taking the time to simply listen and understand what they want to achieve over the long term. It is natural to assume everyone simply wants to climb the ladder, but this is rarely the case. There will be some in the team who have big ambitions and want to be CEO someday. There will be some who simply want to get better at what they currently do. Others will have ambitions of moving sideways into another field or department. There will be others who have no ambitions at all. For them, this is purely a job, and they simply want to do what is required, get paid, and go home and spend time with their family and/or a hobby. Once you understand what everyone wants, it is going to be relatively easy for you to put together a development plan for each of the teams over the next 3 years. It will also make your succession planning efforts a lot easier as you will have a roadmap for where everyone in the organisation plans to go.

The glue that holds the professional development programme together (along with many other programmes) is to then embed the development plans into the short- and long-term objectives set for each employee. So, if you have a software developer who one day hopes to be the CTO, their initial 3-year development plan would be for them to move into their first management role. As a part of this, various steps would need to be taken to develop the person to get ready over the next couple of years. This plan might include things such as participating in management training sessions and being given a chance to lead a small project with some even more junior team members to then put those lessons into practice. On top of this, they might be required to mentor or coach some new graduate hires who have joined the team as well. All of this should be inserted into their performance objectives, and they should also be inserted into the performance objectives of their manager as well. The only way a culture of professional development will develop in an environment where it doesn't already exist is if it has a material impact on all parties involved. This means the manager themselves is measured and rewarded or penalised in their own year-end review, pay rise, promotion, and bonus decisions through their own assessment. Likewise, the manager is going to have their own development plan, and this should take a similar route with their own objective setting and also included in their bosses' objectives.

Without this, it will always be seen as a nice to have but not something that anyone really needs to prioritise or give attention to and, therefore, the same problems will continue. It is amazing how tying people's pay reviews, promotion chances, and bonus entitlements to outcomes can create dramatic shifts in behaviour relatively quickly. There is also another reason why linking professional development plans with performance outcomes is necessary. The truth is that not everyone is going to have the ability to realise their professional development objectives. That software developer may want to be CTO, but it might turn out they make a horrible people leader. Their mini project team may hate dealing with them, and they may struggle with the transition from doing to overseeing and therefore fail miserably. It happens. This allows the organisation to have a fail-safe mechanism of ensuring that there is equal opportunity for all to grow, but growth must still be predicated on the actual demonstration of capability and results. Just because someone wants to get promoted into management doesn't mean they should be promoted. As an employer, you should provide them with the opportunity to develop into a manager, but you should only reward them with that promotion if they demonstrate the ability. This is an important nuance and different to the normal corporate environment where growth is wrongly given to those as a reward for performing well in the last role, not because they have demonstrated the ability to do the next.

Build vs Buy

Providing professional development is important to delivering a great employee experience and high levels of engagement as we have discussed. There is also a further, more pragmatic business reason to pursue the strategy as well. It is the only way to ensure a sustainable pipeline of talent for your organisation. Study after study shows that business leaders are increasingly worried about their organisation's ability to attract and/or retain talent. The truth is they should be worried because times have changed. It used to be the case that the employer seemingly had all of the power. They had the perception that they could replace someone without much trouble. This helped reinforce a culture that people were lucky to be employed, and it didn't matter whether or not the organisation treated the person well. But times have changed, and in the modern economy, the truth is that there are more jobs available than people with the skills to perform them. This has shifted the balance of power to the employees. If they are not happy, they know they have other options.

A lot has been written about 'The Great Resignation' in the past couple of years, but this isn't a post-pandemic issue. As I outline in my book *The Talent Acquisition Handbook*, in December 2018, the United States had 7 million job openings, but only 6.3 million people in the country were unemployed. This was not just vacancies for fancy technology or other STEM-related professions either. These unfilled vacancies were for cooks, cleaners, retail workers, call centre operators, and other essential but lower-paid jobs. There were simply not enough people available with the relevant skills to perform the jobs available. This is also not a US-only problem. It is a global problem. According to Manpower's talent shortage report, there is also a skills shortage of 89% in Japan, 56% in both Singapore and India, 19% in the UK, 51% in Germany, and 13% in China—to name just a few countries. These figures relate only to existing needs. When adding on all of the future capabilities that are going to be needed in the world of 5G and the Internet of Things, the situation looks even bleaker. For example, there are only circa 25 million software engineers in the world, and while that might seem a lot on paper, it is basically the equivalent of the population of Australia or Taiwan. There is clearly no way that Australia or Taiwan could fill all of the software engineering positions in the world.

This reality, whether businesses want to accept it or not, means they are confronted with a clear choice. They can either continue to rely on trying to buy readymade talent from elsewhere, or they can build their own talent. Historically, the approach to expanding a business was relatively simple; you just hired more people. If you wanted to boost sales, then you would simply hire more salespeople. If you were struggling to process all of the sales, then you simply hired more back-office people, and so on and so forth. But those times are now gone. If you do want to buy ready-made talent, you are going to have to pay a significant premium to bring them in. You are going to be competing with multiple other companies, and the consequences are that you will need to pay a lot more. This then has the impact of upsetting your own internal dynamics because the people you are bringing in are paid more, so now your internal people are upset as they aren't paid as much. They will then end up leaving, and then you have to pay even more to bring in even more external talent. To make it worse, not only are they more expensive, but due to the lack of talent, it is likely that you lose up to 9 months of productivity as you look to hire, get someone in, and get them up to speed. Then to make matters worse, it is only 50/50 as to whether or not the new hire stays with the organisation for more than 18 months.

The solution to this challenge should be self-evident. If you cannot rely on finding the talent externally or being able to afford it, then you will have to build the talent yourself. The most common excuses or reasons for not doing this are that it will take too long or cost too much, but both arguments are not based in fact. The evidence actually shows that it's cheaper and quicker to build talent as opposed to buying it. It will typically take around

3 months to upskill an internal member of staff to take on a new set of duties. By contrast, it has been proven repeatedly that it takes 6–9 months to ensure a new external hire is onboarded and fully up to speed. This is because it is not just about acquiring the skill set; the new hire also has to learn the new organisation. They might have experience doing the job elsewhere but have never worked in your organisation. Therefore, someone needs to take the time to show them what the processes and procedures are in your company. They need to be shown what the approval processes are, who can and can't approve things, and so on. On top of this, they will then need to be shown how to use whatever systems and tools your company use. In addition, there might be a project for a new system, and so they need to be included in those meetings going forward and also need to be given a download on the project to date. They will also need to understand the structure of the new team and company and how everyone fits in. Every company is the same but different, and this is why it takes 6–9 months for someone to be fully productive after joining from outside, even if they have the right skills.

In addition to being quicker for these reasons, it is also cheaper. For example, it would typically cost about $20,000 in a developed market to retrain someone as a software engineer. This would be a lot cheaper than hiring a software engineer from outside, where in a developed market, they could command a salary in excess of $100,000. In fact, the recruitment fee is likely to be more than the retraining fee! Then to top it all off, it has been shown that a new hire is 2–3 times more likely to lead to attrition than an internal employee who has been given a development opportunity. This is also a conservative set of estimates. There is research that shows it can cost up to six times more to fill vacancies with external talent that is bought as opposed to internal talent that is built. So, if you want to not only deliver a great employee experience but also create a culture of high engagement and being strong talent pipelines and ensure vacancies are filled more quickly and with a better ROI, then building talent is the way to go.

Coaching

If you want to create an employee-centric culture that enables high engagement and performance levels, then you have to understand what your employees would like. And there is one message that consistently comes through, which is that an employee wants a coach, not a boss. There are fundamental differences between the two, and the truth is that most organisations are structured to enable bosses and not coaches. The traditional command and control, top-down approach of organisational leadership, creates hierarchy and bosses, not coaches and high performance. A boss is someone who is tasked with telling someone what to do, whereas a coach sees it as their responsibility to provide them with the tools to do it. A boss is focused on making sure tasks are completed; a coach utilises the strengths and weaknesses of the team to ensure they are delivered in the best possible way. A boss corrects or punishes mistakes by employees; a coach sees mistakes as learning opportunities to improve performance.

The easiest way to think about coaching is with the famous saying: 'Give a man a fish, and you feed him for a day. Teach a man to fish, and you feed him for a lifetime'. The mistake many organisations make is that they think they are teaching an employee to fish when in reality, all they are doing is giving them the fish. This is because they continually give their people the answers, and by providing their staff with the answers all of the time, they fail to teach them self-reliance. Rather than teaching the team how to fish, they are taught simply to ask the boss, and they will tell them what to do. Some very insecure and mediocre managers and leaders like this because they feel it will keep them in a job as it's clear that as the manager, they are needed because the team do not know what to do without them. This is not how you develop staff or create a highly capable team that are able to outperform. In fact, it often prevents the team from performing at even a basic level. What happens if there is an emergency, and the boss is on annual leave or even just out to lunch or in a meeting? The team sit around and wait for them to come back because they do not know what to do. They have never had to figure anything out for themselves!

To be an effective coach, one of the most powerful questions to ask your people is: 'What do you think you should do?' as this puts the onus back on the member of staff to think through solutions. The tone of this answer is obviously important. There is a big difference between a benevolent coach encouraging someone under their wing to ideate and an awful boss telling a staff member it's their problem and they are on their own. The aim is to be more Mr Miyagi in *The Karate Kid,* and less Meryl Streep in *The Devil Wears Prada.* The aim should be to avoid giving a direct answer at all costs and instead act more like a psychologist and aim to answer any questions with a question. Questions such as 'Why do you think that would work?', 'What could be the downside to that approach?', 'Are there any other ways you could achieve the same outcome?', 'Would this impact any other teams?', 'Do you know anyone that has experienced a similar problem?' and many others should become second nature to your coaches. By refusing to provide the answer directly, you force your employees to figure things out for themselves. They will have to think through all the possible courses of action and their consequences and then decide what they believe is the right one. This simple act is extremely powerful and is the core of the coaching journey within a business. It empowers staff and helps them feel they can figure things out on their own simply by thinking things through logically and leveraging their own experience and that of those around them.

In addition to not providing the answers, there is something else organisations sometimes have to do to coach effectively, and it is something that makes a lot of decision-makers uncomfortable. You have to let a member of staff fail. Failure is often the best teaching mechanism. So, letting a member of staff try a couple of different methods that fail before stumbling onto the right method that succeeds is extremely helpful. Not only will they learn how to do something, but they will also learn why other methods are not as effective. This is something else that is often lost on staff when they are being taught. Their boss has the advantage of experience—they will have likely tried several methods and learnt which ones have worked and haven't worked. But by simply telling your staff to do it one way, which is the way that will work, it always leads to staff insisting it can be done another way that you know will fail. The boss will insist it should be done their way, and the staff become difficult, thinking the boss is being stubborn by insisting it has to be done that way. In reality, all they are trying to do is to save them the wasted effort and to share their experience. Unfortunately, humans are not wired that way.

Coaching is often like parenting. You can tell your infant not to touch the paint on the wall because it is wet. If you have kids, you already know what the child is going to do. They are going to touch it anyway when you are not looking and then get in trouble for making a huge mess. Sometimes the only way to learn why something shouldn't be done is to experience the pain of why it shouldn't be done. With that being said, you should, of course, aim to step in and stop any disasters. I hope there isn't a parent anywhere that would intentionally let their child touch boiling water to learn a lesson about why they shouldn't touch it. Likewise, if you see a member of staff is going to make a huge mistake that could be damaging to the company or your team, you should step in and intervene. But failure is without a doubt the best teacher and when they fail, avoid saying, 'I told you so'.

Instead, support them after the failure, encourage them to try again, and apply what they learnt from the previous attempt so they can figure it out for themselves. It's important not to slip into 'telling' mode after a failure as it takes away the sense of accomplishment and pride an employee will have by figuring it out themselves. The confidence an employee gains from figuring it out themselves is a great catalyst for further growth. They wanted to do something and didn't know how, but they sought some guidance, figured it out, and achieved it. They will then take this into the next task and believe they have the power to do more. This leads to a happy employee who has also become a more productive employee. Everyone wins.

In order to embed a culture of coaching within the organisation, you have to start with the management within the organisation. Are you picking up on a common theme yet? All employee experience is led by their day-to-day interactions with their own manager. It is, therefore, vital that coaching skills are built into the management capability development programmes that should be running all year for the organisation's management group. The good news is that there is so much infrastructure around coaching capability that it is pretty easy to set up a course. The International Coaching Federation (ICF) provides full accreditations and frameworks, and by simply heading over to Google, you will find millions of search results for partners to work with to build formal coaching capability.

With that being said, it is important to remember that just because you have given your managers some training and a certificate does not mean the job is done. There are plenty of folks with Agile or Design Thinking certificates that never put those skills into practice either. So, if you do go down the formal certification route, it is important that it is combined with plenty of practical application within each of the manager's teams, monitoring and assessment, and so on. This is easily done by ensuring coaching objectives are part of each manager's performance assessment and appraisal. Also, remember that you don't need to put all of your managers through formal certification programmes for them to be effective coaches. Elon

Musk, Jeff Bezos, and Mark Zuckerberg don't have MBAs, which didn't stop them from building great businesses. Likewise, your managers don't need a certificate to become great coaches.

Once the organisational coaching programme has equipped its management group with the tools needed to effectively coach, it is obviously time to put it into action with the staff. But it is important to remember that not all employees want or need to be coached. So, it is important that prior to coaching beginning, there is a calibration to align the coaching programme with the development plans of each team member. There are employees who have no desire to be managers but who want to instead become an expert within their field. There are employees who want to switch to other industries. There are others who want their boss's job and some who want to simply pay the bills and be home with the family every night at a reasonable hour. All employees are different, and without actually understanding where they want to go, you can't help them to get there. If you try to coach someone to go in a direction they do not want to go, then rather than building a high performing team and culture, you are going to cause disengagement across the organisation.

Once this alignment with the development plans of each team member is complete, there should be a further breakdown as to who may or may not need coaching. For example, two members of staff may have a development plan to become a technical expert, but their personality traits could vary wildly. One of them may be a proactive and driven individual that is actively pursuing growth on their own. This means they have signed up for extra training courses on their own time, always reach out to colleagues for advice, and so on. This person may need very little coaching. This is not because they don't have a career plan or have all of the answers, but they are very clearly investing in themselves, and so coaching will help, but they are already figuring things out on their own, which is what you want. On the other hand, there is likely to be a member of staff that says they want to be a technical expert but who has never signed up for any training or asked anyone for any advice. Instead, they simply continue to do the same things in the same way unless they are told to do something differently. This is the type of person who can benefit from coaching and being provided with the tools to become self-sufficient. It may seem counterintuitive because the first person is clearly a better bet for future success, but that is the point; they don't need coaching for that exact reason. Helping that person go from knowing 80% to 90% is not as impactful as helping the other person go from 30% to 80%.

The anchor to then measure success, as always, will be for this coaching to be built into the performance objectives of the person being coached, as well as the manager who is obviously coaching. As discussed previously, this is for two reasons. The first is that it provides the employee with a purpose which should lead to higher engagement and performance. The second is that almost everyone claims to be ambitious and wants to do more, but the difference between those who achieve and those that do not is in their actions. So, a person may claim they want a promotion or to become a technical expert, but if they then fail to attend the coaching sessions or take on board the suggestions and continue to do things how they have always been done—then they are not going to be rewarded with that next step. They have not shown they are able to step up to the next level. This would not be a subjective assessment based on opinion, but an objective assessment based on fact resulting from regular coaching and dialogue throughout the year. The aim of professional development is to ensure you take the horse to water, but whether or not the horse drinks is out of your control. Equal opportunity does not mean everyone has equal levels of capability.

Mentorship

As we have discussed, employees are significantly happier and more productive when they feel aligned with the purpose of an organisation and actively contribute towards something larger than themselves, as opposed to just doing a job. This is a universal truth that has been confirmed by numerous pieces of research. It is the core of why great employee experience and the culture of engagement it creates leads to businesses making two and a half times more money than others. But what has often been overlooked is the role mentorship programmes can play in bridging the gap between employee and organisation to achieve this outcome. This is often because they assume a person's manager acts as both a mentor and coach, but this rarely is the case.

Coaching is best used to address performance-related issues. Someone is performing a job function, and in order to improve performance, there are additional things that can be enhanced. So, a coach would help the employee to improve and develop to perform better. This is why coaching is such an important people management trait. If a manager wants to succeed, they have to be able to coach their people, and if the organisation wants to succeed, then all of its managers must be able to coach. Mentorship, on the other hand, is much more long term and is best provided by someone senior who is not directly managing the person. This is because the direct manager usually lacks the required capability to provide long-term mentorship for an employee. For example, if we revert to the example of a software developer that would like to become CTO—how can their boss, the software development manager, mentor this person on what needs to be done to become CTO? They can't. They have never been a CTO themselves. It would be much more helpful for the CTO to actually provide mentorship directly to help this person understand how they became CTO, the challenges they faced, and the hurdles they overcame to get there.

This is why corporate mentorship programmes are becoming more mainstream. It is a great way to link short-term goals with long-term goals. That software developer is not going to become CTO in the next couple of years, but by being able to seek advice and guidance from the CTO regularly, they know there is a long-term reason to stick around. The organisation is helping them to work on their long-term aspirations, and at the same time, they are still being coached and focused on delivering on the short-term objectives. After all, they aren't going to be on the path to CTO if they can't succeed in their current role. The benefits of corporate mentorship programmes are also significant. A well-known technology company that is a member of the Fortune 500 found that employees who participated in such programmes were 5 times more likely to be promoted than those who did not. It also found that the senior people who were providing the mentoring were 6 times more likely to be promoted as well. In addition to this, they also discovered that retention rates for both mentors and mentees also increased by 70%.

However, for an organisational mentorship programme to deliver such benefits, it is important for some foundational criteria to be in place. There are some very clear differences between organisations that run successful mentorship programmes and those that do not. The starting point for ensuring a programme is a success is that it absolutely must be a voluntary programme. It is vital that the corporate mentorship programme does not become another mandatory HR training programme that staff and management are obliged to attend. Mentorship is an important but also time-consuming activity. Therefore, the people who are part of the programme must actually want to be part of the programme. Without this voluntary element to the programme everything else falls apart, and you will not deliver a successful programme.

The reason for this is simple. If you force a leader to be a mentor, how fruitful do you think that experience is going to be for a mentee? If they have zero desire to be part of the programme, are they going to be making themselves available regularly and going out of their way to ensure the mentee is supported? Of course not. So, the experience of the mentee is going to be very negative, and rather than enhancing employee experience and engagement, you are going to do the opposite. The mentee is going to feel very unimportant and become disengaged. Likewise, the mentor is not going to be happy they are being forced to spend time mentoring some people they really don't want to. This doesn't make the senior leader a bad person. Senior people have demanding jobs; they have family commitments, may be part of other social, sporting, or community groups, and have even more commitments on top of family and work. That's life.

The same is also true in the reverse scenario. If you have a senior leader who is very keen to become a mentor and share their journey and experience with the next generation, giving them a mentee that doesn't want to be there is also pointless. The member of staff is only there because they are being forced to and they don't want to learn, which leads to them being further disengaged. Similarly, the senior leader is thinking the entire mentor programme is a waste of time because the people being assigned to them clearly don't value or respect the time the mentor is giving up. Thus, for the programme to be a success, it must be a voluntary programme. A mentor must want to mentor, and a mentee must want to learn. Without this important first step, your mentor programme is doomed before it has begun. This might mean the programme starts out small. But it is better to start small with a group of people who have volunteered and want it to be a success. It is more likely to succeed instead of rolling it out companywide with a load of people who don't want to support it.

In addition to the programme being voluntary, there are other hurdles to overcome. Once you have identified the participants in the voluntary programme as both mentor and mentee, the next step is to focus on matching the individuals who are part of the programme. Remember, just because someone is willing to mentor and someone is willing to be a mentee does not mean that specific mentor should be paired with that specific mentee. As we have discussed elsewhere in this book, everyone has different personalities and objectives. This is why it is important to align the personalities and objectives of both mentor and mentee. Quite simply, if you pair a mentee who is looking to develop into an industry-leading expert with a mentor who is not an industry-leading technical expert, then the programme is not going to succeed. The mentor doesn't need to be a technical expert in the same field; after all, that is where coaching comes in. But the mentor does need to be able to share how they became a technical expert in their own respective field. Likewise, if you pair a mentor who wants to help others develop leadership skills with someone who does not want to be a leader, the programme is not going to be successful.

One of the best ways to mitigate the chances of misalignment is to ensure that there is some sort of questionnaire and interview as part of voluntarily signing up for the programme. This allows the team to get a clear picture of what each person is looking to get out of the programme. This should also be combined with some sort of psychometric profiling tool that will help you to align personality and working styles. A high-level strategic thinker is not going to gel with a detail-orientated person who wants to ensure bullet point four on page 73 is formatted correctly and vice versa. This doesn't mean either person is a poor performer, but they are not going to be the right fit to connect with each other. How they will approach things will be at odds with what the other person would be comfortable doing. You can be successful either way, but an introvert is not going to feel comfortable taking an extrovert's opinion that they have to spend lots of time networking with strangers. It would be much more useful for them to understand how another introvert made it to the top and navigated needing to build a network while being naturally introverted.

Next comes the third and final element that differentiates organisations that have successful corporate mentorship programmes and those not relating to the structure of the programme. It is important to remember that there is no one-size-fits-all approach to mentorship. Many mentorship programmes fall into the trap of enforcing an arbitrary time limit or meeting cadence on the participants. They might insist that the mentor and mentee need to meet once a week for an hour for a duration of 3 months or 6 months. This approach is pointless and consistently fails. This is because it is not contextual to the objectives of the mentor and mentee. If we revert to the example of the software developer who one day wants to become CTO, there is very little value in the software developer meeting the CTO for an hour each week for 3 or 6 months. Becoming CTO is a long-term goal. It would be much more valuable for the software developer to maybe have a two-hour lunch with their senior leader mentor once a quarter to pick their brain and get some guidance. It is going to take them years to become CTO, so having 12 meetings in 12 weeks is not going to be useful. On the flip side, an hour a week may not be enough for someone looking to become a technical expert. It might be more useful for that person to shadow their mentor as they work on a specific project to see the approach they take to develop and apply their skills. So, remember to ensure the programme has agility and flexibility built in to cater to the needs of the participants. It will greatly increase the likelihood of the programme being a success.

Training

Once the organisation has development plans in place for all employees and are able to combine this with regular coaching and mentoring, the employee experience and engagement levels should be heading in the right direction. However, no development programme can be complete without additional training to teach new capabilities. But there is an important nuance to training; it has to be relevant and practical in order to be useful. Unfortunately, many organisations think merely sending a member of staff to a training course means that they have provided their people with development. This is not the case. The organization usually sends someone off to a training course where they will get a certificate they will never use. Harvard Business Review found that despite organisations spending in excess of $400 billion a year on external training programmes, only 12% of those who attend the training apply what they learn in their jobs. In addition, research from McKinsey shows that only 25% of those who attended training felt that it improved performance. What is fascinating about this is that despite research consistently showing that organisations are spending significant sums of money on training, 70% of employees feel they do not have the required skills to perform at their full potential.

There is a key reason for this disconnect between organisations providing training and employees saying they don't have the required skills. The reason is that employees are often sent away on a training course, and they learn all of these wonderfully complex frameworks and methodologies, and then when they return to the office, they have no idea how to apply those principles internally within their own roles within the company. This is why it is so important that an organisation's training strategy is broken down into two categories of training. The first is training that can be conducted internally, and the second is training that should be conducted externally. To ensure that your employees reap the benefits of training and find it useful, you need to ensure that you get the balance right. External training will always be fancier and more formal, but that doesn't always mean it's better. In fact, the informal and less well-structured internal training programmes often significantly outperform the more formal external training programmes.

As a rule of thumb, internal training programmes should always be the first option over external training programmes. The key reason for this is that while external training programmes are significantly more comprehensive, they are unable to provide context for how to apply the principles learned within the organisation. For example, if you work for an old-fashioned insurance company, you can send your people to attend a workshop on innovation principles run by Google, but your people are not going to use them. Don't get me wrong, your people will probably love learning all of Google's innovation principles, but the old-fashioned insurer isn't Google. So, whilst your people have enjoyed the training, they are also thinking, 'Dude, of course, Google can do all of this stuff; they are Google—in our company, my boss still prints out emails to read as hard copies, how am I going to use this stuff?' Therefore, while the people will enjoy the session, they haven't bought into the idea of being able to do it internally because the training does not take into account the internal dynamics of the organisation and how to navigate that to ensure the principles can be applied.

Research shows that the best communicators and trainers are not those who explain every single aspect of a methodology or a process. The best trainers are those who know what information to leave out. This is where internal training often outperforms external training. This is because, assuming you have someone internally within your organisation who understands the principles involved in whatever concept is being taught, they are able to share what their colleagues need to know. This is a lot more powerful than sharing every single aspect of a topic. It allows for the relevant information to be absorbed, and because the person providing the training works for the company, they can contextualise it to the organisation. This is something I have done myself when leading training sessions on design thinking for organisations I have worked for. To become certified in the topic, I sat through several days of painstaking training going through slide after slide of methodology. However, I can train pretty much anyone to understand and apply design thinking principles in about 20 minutes. Most people don't need to understand the entire history of design thinking. They just need to know there are 5 key steps, why they are important, and how they can implement them.

This is why internal training is often the better starting point. It provides those in the organisation a decent baseline and understanding at scale and then those who really need to become technical experts in an area to then move into more formal training. But the truth is that most people don't need a certificate.

174

They just need a practical understanding of what a concept is and how they can use it to deliver better results. The best people to share that are often colleagues who are already using the principles in the existing organisation. In addition to internal training being able to accommodate better for organisational culture, the trainers are often more relatable, which also helps the effectiveness of the training. This is because the people who are leading the training sessions are employees of the same organisation. This means they should be sharing real-life examples, problems, and challenges that all employees within the company can relate to on a day-to-day basis. An existing employee sharing with others how they have taken a different approach to successfully overcome these challenges is very powerful. It is very hard for someone to claim, 'that wouldn't work here', or 'that's not how we do it' when it does, in fact, work here, and that is how other teams who are getting better results are doing it. They can also explain it while using internal language and referring to internal dynamics, which is a key reason why such training programmes are more impactful than traditional external training programmes. This also gives employees confidence that the desired outcomes can be achieved because one of their colleagues has already done it.

This, of course, doesn't mean that there is no place for external training, quite the opposite. External training can provide a great return on investment, but only when it is used properly. As a general rule, external training should be used in two main scenarios. The first, as already shared, is when you have set a baseline internally and then want to augment that knowledge with more complex frameworks and methodologies. The second is when the organisation lacks the required capability internally to facilitate internal training. An example of where you might want to set a baseline internally and then augment it with external expertise could be in your accounting team. Most finance teams will consist of some individuals who are qualified accountants and others who are not. It would therefore make sense to have the folks who are qualified accountants share knowledge internally regularly with the non-qualified members of staff to help them perform better. At the same time, for individuals whose development plans involve them advancing up the ladder and taking on more responsibility, it would also make sense to ensure they are enrolled in a formal programme to get their accounting certifications. An example of going straight to external training would be for a team that is implementing a new system. As none of the existing team had worked with the system before, there is no one to share some knowledge, and so they would need to be formally trained elsewhere.

As your organisation look to engage external training partners, you should always aim to stick to a principle of learning when it is needed. Internal training is able to serve multiple purposes. It is not just about teaching new skills but also reinforcing culture, ways of working, organisational values and principles, and so on. It should be part of an ongoing attempt to shape the organisation. External training, on the other hand, is often simply about learning a new topic. The history of humanity shows that most people do not learn because they should; they learn when they need to. Therefore, sending your workforce on a digital transformation programme when no digital transformation plans or programmes exist for them to work on is doomed to fail. You might want your people to learn those skills because they are valuable. But as far as your employees are concerned, it's not something they need to learn; it's something you are forcing them to learn. It is often a waste of time. This is because if they are not going to be able to put those principles into practice immediately, then they are going to forget them. In fact, research by the Harvard Business Review shows that an individual will forget about 75% of what they have learned if they do not physically apply it within 6 days of learning it. So, it's important to ensure there is an immediate need to apply what they have learned. Without this, employees do not see the experience as worthwhile, and you will not see a return on investment.

This brings us to the final step to ensuring the training programmes deliver the required results. It is vital there is a clear follow-up strategy and plan in place for execution once the training session has been completed. Far too many organisations send their people away on training and then never follow up. If they do not have tangible action points to work on within the week after training, then they are going to forget most of what they learned. HR or management teams will often say, 'Well, they should know how to do something because we gave them some training'. It is a completely unrealistic expectation. If you take a group of people who have done things a certain way for a decade, spend two hours showing them another way of doing something, and then just expect them to start doing it, you are deluded. It is never going to happen. Instead, there needs to be consistent follow up and a clear timeline for implementing the new ideas and concepts they have been taught. Quite simply, if there is no plan of action, then there will be no action.

The easiest way to do this is to link the need to learn with performance objectives. The approach required is very similar to ensuring your coaching, mentoring, and overall development plans for staff become a reality. They have to be linked to tangible, measurable outcomes that impact everyone's performance review, promotion, pay rise, and bonus chances, not just for the employee but also for their manager. So, if you were to send a member of HR on a design thinking course, there must be a tangible need for them to acquire these skills, and this must be tied into a specific problem to solve that can be measured as a performance objective. An easy use case could be for the employee to then be tasked with taking their newly acquired design thinking skills and being tasked with creating a programme to improve engagement scores by 5% in next year's survey.

Alternatively, it might be that a software developer has learnt a new software language, and they are tasked with both delivering a project using the new software and also creating a knowledge-sharing programme to help upskill other team members. This allows employees to put their skills to use and allows your employees to get the most out of the training. Not only are they applying the skills they have learned, proving that the training was valuable, but they will also gain confidence from the success achieved as a result of delivering a project using the new skills. They will see the impact almost immediately. This will encourage them to continue to apply such skills in future and also seek out additional new skills to help them further. But if you cannot find a tangible link between need and a business outcome, you should be questioning why you are sending the person on the training course to begin with.

Retraining

As we have discussed throughout this book, one of the biggest challenges facing organisations is a lack of talent with the required skills. In fact, when organisations are asked about their ability to meet the demands of the ever-growing digital world, they consistently say they lack the required capabilities. Most companies will tell you they are struggling to hire the right talent as there is a global skills shortage. To make matters worse, this skills shortage is only going to be further exacerbated as the years go on, and more and more companies are competing for a small pool of skilled individuals. Yet, there seems to be a statistic that has often been overlooked and gone unnoticed as businesses discuss how they are going to meet the talent needs of the future. That is the number of people who are going to have an obsolete skill set. I do not think it's a surprise that the proposed number of positions that will go unfilled as a result of a talent shortage is almost identical to the number of people who will potentially lose their jobs because their skill set will become obsolete.

This is because roles are changing. Technology will continue to take over the role of low-level skills; it always has and always will. But technology rarely takes away employment altogether. Roles change; they do not disappear. In fact, research shows that new technology usually creates more vacancies than it eliminates. Major disruption is nothing new. This digital revolution we are currently going through is, in fact, the fourth time humanity has experienced what could be termed the future of work. This is the fourth industrial revolution. If you look back through history, there is a common theme throughout each shift brought about by technological change. The only losers are those who refuse to change. For example, over 200 years ago in the USA, 90% of workers worked on a farm. Today roughly 2% do. Despite this, at no point were 88% of Americans unemployed. Roles changed, and society shifted, but there are significantly more Americans employed today than over 200 years ago. This is a familiar story the world over. Technological change frees up the capacity for workers to learn new skills that create more value. Now, as businesses aim to survive this major disruption for the fourth time, the roadmap to doing so should not only be obvious, but they can also greatly improve employee experience while doing it. The way to achieve this is simple—to retrain existing employees and provide them with new skills to thrive in the new world.

However, despite this being one of the most obvious ways for an organisation to ensure it is able to build sustainable pipelines of talent, organisations are often reluctant to do so. There are a number of obstacles to overcome in order to retrain staff. The first of these, and one of the most damning statistics when it comes to learning and development programmes, is that training is overwhelmingly skewed toward the young. Research from the Department of Labour discovered that workers aged 25–34 receive, on average, 37 hours of training a year, whereas workers aged 55 and above receive only 7 hours of training per year. It does not take a genius to realise that this is a core reason why the older generation are lacking the skills to thrive as technological advancement happens. Career development does not stop when someone reaches their mid-30s, but when it comes to training and development, it appears most organisations seem to think it does. It should be no surprise that organisations are struggling to find enough talent with the required skills when they are actively underinvesting in their experienced workers. This is also not just an issue for the over 55s. The same research shows that people in their 40s also receive less training than their younger peers.

This issue is also at the core of why so many organisations are struggling to adapt to the shifting sentiment of customers. It is also why so many businesses are desperately trying to (and usually failing to) go through a digital transformation. An organisation's older workers are more likely to make up the management and leadership ranks. Therefore, if these groups are being provided with less training, this means that their ways of working are not going to keep up to date. So, they will naturally keep on doing things the way they have always been done because no one is showing them any other way to do things. This then leads to outdated practices and stagnating business results, which will naturally lead to declining results. At the same time, it is these leaders and managers that are meant to be coaching, mentoring, and training their younger members of staff. Yet, how are they supposed to do this if the organisation is not taking the time to first train and upskill them?

There are those that will point the finger at the older generation and claim they are stuck in their ways and don't want to change. But that kind of blanket statement is pure bias and discrimination. Are there some older workers that don't want to learn anything new? Yes. Are there some younger workers that don't want to learn anything new? Yes. It is not an age problem; it is a mindset problem. The truth is that most older workers want to learn new skills, and research backs this up. It has been shown that 8 out of 10 employees aged 45–64 say that a job where they can learn new skills is important to them. A further 7 out of 10 say that ongoing training is crucial to keeping them engaged in their job. Older workers are very keen to learn new skills. The problem is rarely a lack of desire but instead a lack of opportunity that prevents them from doing so.

So much has been said and written about the multigenerational workforce in the past decade, and to be honest, most of it is complete nonsense. The majority of what has been said and written consists of the following 2 stereotypes: Millennials and Gen Zs are all technologically savvy but also entitled and impatient and impossible to keep happy. Baby boomers are all old and resistant to change and would still use a typewriter if they could. Then there are usually a few sentences added in relation to Generation X being stuck in the middle between the old generation and the new. All of this is nothing more than sweeping generalisations and also one of the key reasons why organisations are struggling to build an effective multigenerational workforce. The truth is that an organisation's ability to build an effective workforce has very little to do with the age of its workers and everything to do with the mindset of its workers.

One of my favourite statistics to combat this sweeping sense of generalisation and stereotyping relates to job hopping. It doesn't take long to find a leader or manager within an organisation who will tell you that these youngsters today just jump from job to job and there is no loyalty anymore. But do you want to know a fun fact? It isn't true. Millennials and Gen Zs do not change jobs more often than other generations. This has been confirmed and validated by numerous pieces of research. The truth is that those who are a bit older and further along in their careers have forgotten what they wanted early on in their careers. In fact, Deloitte found that the retention rates of younger staff now are almost identical to what it was 30 years ago. Employees who are early in their careers naturally want to gain more experience and progress and grow a lot faster than people who have been building their careers for the last 10/15/20 years. This means that those earlier on in their career move more often. They always have, and they always will. Broadly speaking, the younger generation is looking for knowledge and new experiences, not security and stability.

This has always been a fact of life and continues to be so. The same types of leaders and organisations currently complaining about those millennials and Gen Z members would have been complaining about the kids starting their careers in the 1980s or 1990s as well. But there is something else that has always been true. If an organisation or leaders provides their people with a true career path, consistent learning, and development opportunities, they will retain talent better than their peers. They will also have better levels of engagement, performance, and employee experience. This is universally true regardless of generation, geography, or industry. A person's age does not dictate how they behave; instead, it is often more a combination of their own personality combined with their life stage. A 25-year-old that got married at 18 and has 3 kids is more likely to behave like a stereotypical person in their 40s. Likewise, someone who is in their 40s and is unmarried and childless and starting a new career will have more in common with a stereotypical person in their early 20s. This is why it is so important to ensure that career development is tailored to the wants and needs of each individual rather than a blanket approach. The same is true of your efforts to retrain workers.

The success or failure of your efforts to retrain staff will depend a lot more on whether a staff member has a fixed or growth mindset as opposed to how old they are. Plenty of folks over 50 are up to date with the latest trends. There are also plenty of younger people that struggle to adapt to change. This is the real issue at the core of organisations' efforts to successfully undergo transformation, which is essentially what you are doing as you begin to retrain staff to perform new roles. Those who are more likely to want to learn and try new things will have growth mindsets, and those who are reluctant to do so are more likely to have fixed mindsets. Ironically, those who perpetuate the myth of certain generations or demographics being a certain way are displaying a fixed belief associated with a fixed mindset. While some generalisations might hold true at a macro level—e.g., perhaps 60% of a certain demographic are more inclined to want to vote for one political party over another—this doesn't mean everyone in that demographic will. The same is true of every other aspect, including a desire and ability to be retrained in a new field.

The final obstacle that often holds back organisations from investing in retraining their older workers is the mistaken belief that older workers won't be around for long. Just as with the belief that older workers don't want to learn new things or are incapable of learning new things, this is incorrect. This belief is often based on an assumption that workers would either retire soon or simply be too unhealthy to work for longer. Many would argue it is not worth investing in people in their 50s, let alone their 60s. Research shows these views are incorrect. In fact, over the last generation, life expectancy has increased by 5–10 years in most developed countries. The number of employees continuing to work past their 70th birthday has doubled over the past decade, and it is a number that is going to continue to grow. Older workers are actually the fastest-growing part of the workforce. The Department of Labour anticipates a further 55% growth in the 65–74 employment demographic over the coming few years, while the rest of the workforce is only expected to grow by 5%.

Investing in retraining workers in their 50s or even 60s makes more sense, as employers are likely to get another 10–20 years of service out of these employees. Further research shows that older workers are less likely to change jobs than those earlier in their careers. Therefore, you are actually more likely to see a better return on your investment by retraining older members of the workforce. This obviously doesn't mean you should only retrain older workers, just like you shouldn't only train younger workers—retraining should be based on role as opposed to age. But if someone needs to be retrained, by definition, it means that they are likely to be older as they have to have been trained to do something else before they can be retrained. So, how do you embark on retraining staff?

This may seem obvious, but the key to successfully retraining staff is to start by identifying both the relevant and obsolete skills a team or department will need upfront. I say this may seem obvious, but very few organisations go through this process on a regular basis. Just as very few managers or HR teams can show you a 3-year development plan for each employee, the same is true for their own department's business plan. Retraining begins where career development and business planning meet. But in order to retrain, there must be a career development and business plan. Most organisations' business plan stops at 'well, next year we need to hit these sales figures'. Business planning is supposed to go far beyond the simple financial plan for the organisation. The financial plan should be linked to the organisational strategy, and each department should have a clear road map for how their own department needs to evolve over the next 3 years in order to deliver on the plan. Unless your organisation is a start-up, a plan that simply involves hiring more people to do the exact same things in the exact same way is a terrible plan. There needs to be an evolution. Better processes, systems, tools, and ways of working should all be part of the business plan that enables the realisation of both the financial plan and business strategy.

So, for example, a plan for the finance team may mean shifting from managing the accounts manually in Excel to using some sort of accounting system. A plan for the customer service team may mean an increased use of chatbots. Both of these would then require the existing team to pivot. Someone in the finance team may find they are no longer needed as the new system will mean that fewer people are required to manually enter and maintain all of the data. Likewise, an increase in chatbots would mean that fewer front-line customer service personnel may be needed. This then means there is an opportunity to retrain. The current roles may not be required anymore, but new ones will be. A person may not be required to enter the data into Excel, but someone will now need to look at the reports from the new accounting system, analyse the data, and provide some insights into what it means. So, this presents an opportunity for someone to shift from doing finance admin work to financial analysis work. Similarly, there might be a need for fewer customer service agents, but there would be a need for someone to look at the nature of customer requests, analyse what the most common customer issues are, and then design customer programmes to solve them and improve customer experience. Therefore, this 'as is' and 'to be' mapping of current skills and future skills should be mapped out to design the retraining needs of each department along with the individuals that would be impacted. This is something that should be regularly refreshed as part of the ongoing business planning work an organisation should be doing.

Once the individuals are identified, there is one more step before you jump into action and send them for retraining. This is to calibrate whether or not the retraining is part of their desired career development plan. Another reason why reskilling programmes fail is because the people who are undergoing reskilling have absolutely no desire to be reskilled. This might seem illogical, but as we have discussed, fixed mindsets are common. I once sat on the technology leadership team of a global financial services organisation that was undergoing a huge shift from legacy systems to new modern systems. A significant proportion of the technology team had outdated skills as they were working on systems that had been obsolete for at least a decade. We offered the individuals impacted a chance to be upskilled, and the majority of folks naturally took up the offer. But to our surprise, there were a number of individuals that declined the offer. They did not want to learn to do anything new under any circumstances.

This was especially shocking as they did not have any experience with modern tech platforms. The systems they were working on had been decommissioned by the technology company that made it several years before. They would not be able to find employment elsewhere as no one else was using those systems— it would be the equivalent of being an expert in building a Sega Mega Drive in the 2020s. Sega stopped selling them in the late 1990s! We were offering them the opportunity to learn how to build a Sony PlayStation 5, and they declined. They left our organisation, and when I bumped into one of them a couple of years later, they had still not found another opportunity. This is why it is so important to align your programme with career development plans and to also make the programme voluntary. As the saying goes, you can take a horse to water, but you cannot force it to drink. So, whether it is your mentoring programme, training, or retraining, there is very little benefit in forcing someone to learn something or accept development they do not want.

The good news is that there will be plenty of other employees who will jump at the opportunity to learn something new both internally and elsewhere. But do not waste resources on individuals that don't want it. Once you have aligned the reskilling needs with the career development plans of the individuals in question, you can then send them on to the reskilling programme. Setting up this training should follow a similar pattern to that outlined under the previous section regarding training. Then to ensure the change takes hold and is a success, ensure that it is incorporated into everyone's performance objectives—both employees being reskilled and their managers. This will ensure that everyone is incentivised and rewarded for successfully reskilling.

Chapter 7: Pay & Benefits

If there is one topic that can bring out strong emotions and opinions in the workplace, it is probably a discussion around salary. If I were to make a sweeping generalisation—it often seems like employees feel like they are underpaid, and management feel like staff are overpaid and claim they can't afford to pay them more. But let's be clear: if you want to create a highly engaged workforce, performing to exceptional standards, and delivering outstanding business results, then you need to pay your people fairly. But the keyword here is *fairly*. This is because contrary to popular belief, salary is not the leading factor in ensuring you have a workforce that's highly engaged. Research consistently shows that you only have to pay people a reasonable salary and combine this with a great environment, meaningful work, and career development, and the majority of your people will never leave. I will repeat this again so that I am not misunderstood. You do not need to pay your people the best salary in the world. You need to provide them with a fair salary that is representative of the work they do. If you do this and ensure that your workplace is a good environment that provides its people with meaningful work and career development possibilities, your people are going to be happy.

As I have shared in other chapters and some of my other books, the challenge is rarely to motivate and engage but instead rather not to cause disengagement. The reason why salary is often seen as the source of disengagement is because it is an easy way to recognise the value and contribution of an employee. So, if the standard rate for a position is $50,000 and you are only paying members of staff $25,000, then they are going to be disengaged, and they are going to leave. The truth is they are not leaving because someone else has offered them more money. They are leaving because your organisation has been taking advantage of them and undervaluing the work they were doing. You are essentially cheating your employees. This is what creates a negative employee experience and disengagement. Research shows that if, in the same example, you were paying them $48,000 and the organisation culture is fantastic, employees are learning new skills and doing some meaningful work, then they will be happy. Sure, they would like a bit more money (who wouldn't?), but they know they are relatively fairly paid, and they are learning new skills and doing important work which will help them increase their salary in the future. In addition, they like the company and their colleagues, so why move for a couple of hundred dollars more each month and risk ending up with a bad boss and crap culture? The occasional person will make this decision because maybe they have just found out they are going to have another child and, therefore, will need the extra money—but the research shows this is a minority.

The research also indicates that the reverse is true. You can overpay people, but if they work in a toxic work environment, the majority will not stay regardless of the pay. So, you could pay people $75,000 for a position that is worth $50,000, and it is not going to make a difference to employee experience, engagement, or business results if the environment is bad. Again, this makes perfect sense. Why would someone choose to stay in an environment where their boss is a horrible tyrant, their colleagues are awful people, they aren't doing anything meaningful, and they have zero future career prospects? The majority of people are going to choose to leave. The ones that do choose to stay are going to be the ones that need the pay cheque. They may choose to stay because they need the money, but they are not going to be highly engaged and delivering high performance because the culture will not enable it. So, the priority should be focused on ensuring that salary is fair while building a culture that provides meaningful work and a good environment.

This approach consistently works. In fact, I once personally worked with a client where I helped them to reduce the salary of staff over a 3-year period, and this led to them increasing retention of staff. The company used to pay its people above an average salary, and it had attrition of 25%+ consistently. I worked with them to bring this salary down to an average level and invest the difference in a variety of programmes to improve culture and career development. The result was that even though people were paid less on average, their attrition dropped from 25%+ over the past decade to less than 5% over the next 3 years. People chose to stay because they knew they were fairly paid, and because of the investment in the culture and people's careers, they wanted to stay. They knew they could get a 20% increase in salary by going elsewhere, but they also knew the other company could not match the culture and career opportunities they were now being provided. So, the majority chose to stay. The result was that attrition was now only 4%, and in years 2 and 3, as the programmes really took hold, they delivered the best two years of financial performance in company history.

Salary

The best place to begin to implement a fair pay strategy is with the job offer process. It is a lot easier to ensure your reward processes are fit for purpose by ensuring those who come into the organisation start off on the right foot. The alternative is that your employees either start off disengaged as they feel it is an unfair salary offer, or they come to that realisation pretty early on in their career with your company. Then it is a lot harder, but not impossible, to walk that back. In order to do this, an organisation must ensure its job offer process is aligned to paying people based on their capability. This may seem obvious, but as I outline in my book *The Talent Acquisition Handbook*, the truth is that the majority of organisations make offers based on arbitrary data points such as a person's last salary or their years of experience. Neither of these things have anything to do with a person's level of capability. If you can get this process right, then you will be ahead of 95% of other organisations. This is because most organisations still rely on the lazy, outdated, and fundamentally flawed approach of basing an offer on the person's current salary.

Such an approach is bad because using this approach often means you will underpay a high performer, overpay a low performer, and also discriminate against women and minorities! So, if your organisation takes someone's current salary into consideration as part of the offer process, then this is something you need to stop immediately. The reason the approach of taking a person's previous salary and simply adding a fixed increment on top has a bad impact is easy to understand. Let's start with high performers. High performers progress much faster than others, which is why they are high performers. Their average tenure in a role is circa 18 months as opposed to closer to 3 years for average performers. This means they are promoted faster and, therefore, end up in more senior roles at a younger age. The downside to this is that often, their salary fails to keep up with the rate at which they progress. If someone starts out as a trainee and is paid $20,000 and gets promoted 7 times in 7 years to become a department head, they are likely to be underpaid despite the level of responsibility. If the person were given a 20% pay rise every year, they would still be on less than $72,0000. As a department head, you would expect them to be on at least 50% more than that. Now ask yourself how many companies you know would give a staff member a 20% pay rise every year for 7 years? Thus, high performers who stay with one organisation for a long period of time are often significantly underpaid compared to counterparts who move more often. So, if you simply base an offer on their current salary, you are going to still underpay them, which means they are going to end up leaving when someone else offers them what they are truly worth. This also creates a horrific employee experience because they are going to feel like your organisation is trying to take advantage of them and get them on the cheap. This is also why using other data points, such as years of experience, is a bad idea to just pay for seniority. It means you can never hire or retain high performers as you are always going to undervalue them.

At the same time, low performers who stay with an organisation for the long term are often overpaid. This is because they aren't moving up the ranks but are still getting an annual pay rise. So, despite not being good enough to climb the ladder, they get paid more and more for doing the exact same job. And when they eventually move, they are already on a very high salary for the role they perform. This is also why basing hiring and pay decisions on 'years of experience' is a bad idea. The longer someone has been doing something, the more likely they are to be mediocre or an underperformer. So, if you base an offer on what they are currently paid, then you are going to overpay for their level of ability, and as their poor performance becomes evident, this is going to cause issues in the team. People talk, and so when the team find out this underperformer is one of the highest paid members of the team, you are going to have a lot of your good team members looking for an exit. This practice of simply adding a percentage on top of the current salary is also a key reason why the gender pay gap persists. If a woman is paid 20% less than a male counterpart and you, HR, or the organisation as a whole have a policy of only offering a 10% increase to new joiners, it is impossible for the woman to catch up. This is why there has been so little progress on eradicating the gender pay gap over the past several years despite it receiving so much attention. Similar pay gaps also exist and continue to be perpetuated with minority groups for the same reason.

There is also another process issue that leads to organisations struggling to put together a fair salary package which often leads to a negative employee experience. This is the incorrect use of a compa ratio. The compa ratio itself is an outdated way of creating offers and benchmarking salary as it is over 50 years old by this point. Yet most organisations cling to it religiously in creating their salary benchmarks, leading to them struggling to present a

195

fair package to talent. Most companies will set their compa ratio to the industry's midpoint or, putting it in simpler terms, the average salary. So, the compa ratio would be set at 1.0 at the average salary. However, organisations then make the mistake of thinking they cannot or should not pay above this mark, leading to good talent being unfairly paid and creating a negative experience and disengagement as a result.

This is because the only people who would be able to get a good salary package as a result of joining an organisation with this compa ratio are low performers. For example, if the average salary is $50,000, then this means that an average performer at your organisation or a competitor should already be paid $50,000. So, for any talent to join your organisation, they would expect a pay rise, but most organisations will not offer this as it involves paying above the industry midpoint. Therefore, they set their own budget at $50,000. This then means that the only people that will consider joining is the bottom third of the talent pool because they will be paid a salary equivalent to the bottom third of the budget. For simplicity, this means they are probably paid $30K to 40K, so $50,000 is a pay rise. Meanwhile, top talent is already going to be paid an above-average salary, which leads to companies trying to convince external candidates already on $60,000 that moving for the same money is a good deal. It isn't, and it creates a horrific experience. Especially when the same data will show a top performer in the field is usually paid $80,000. But because the organisation is using a compa ratio set at the industry midpoint, this usually means they would end up in a higher salary band as the salary bands are designed around average pay, and they feel they can't go above that.

This doesn't only hurt new employees who are joining the organisation, but also existing employees' ability to get a fair pay rise at the end of the year. If they are an average employee and are already paid $50,000, then many organisations make the mistake of thinking if they give this person a pay rise, they will be overpaid. So, you end up in a situation where you have an employee who is paid $50,000 who has gained new skills and dramatically increased their performance over the past 12 months, and they are now a top performer. This means that they should be paid somewhere closer to the $80,000 benchmark of top performers in their field. They probably shouldn't get the jump all the way to $80,000 for being a top performer for only one year, but they should be getting a good increase. However, what happens is that an organisation will instead only give them a small increase because the organisation mistakenly believes they can't pay more than the 1.0 compa ratio. This then causes the now high performing talent to become disengaged because they know the company is not being fair. It is fine to have a generic compa ratio midpoint, but when creating a salary package or reviewing salary, the organisation needs to take the entire salary banding into consideration. This means that the midpoint might be $90,000, but the lower rate of $80,000 and a higher point of $100,000 should also be open to consideration. The midpoint is supposed to be a guide for what you pay a run-of-the-mill member of staff performing the role who is average in every way, not a guide for what you are supposed to pay all staff performing that role.

So, your organisation needs to create a salary proposal based on their assessment of the employee against the criteria of the position they have. This means you will either assess them as someone who is a great fit and delivering above and beyond expectations (a top performer), a solid member of staff who does what is asked (an average performer), or someone who has potential but still has a lot to learn (a low performer who will grow over time). Based on this, their salary should be at the top, middle, or bottom of the salary band on offer. This is not the midpoint of the compa ratio but the entire band available from worst performer to best in class. This means if the salary band is $80,000 to $100,000, you would pay someone who comes across as a solid member of staff $90,000, someone who comes across as more junior but with potential $80,000 to $85,000, and someone who comes across as incredibly strong would get $95,000 to $100,000. You are essentially paying them fairly based upon their level of capability.

This means they are more likely to stick around long term and feel like they are treated fairly. It also means they will have a much better employee experience and not feel like they are being screwed over or lowballed purely because of some arbitrary rule. They are instead being properly assessed based on their level of capability, and the salary is aligned to that assessment and nothing else. This means that if you assess someone as a solid employee at $90,000, you pay them $90,000 even if they are currently on $70,000 and say they will be happy with $75,000. There is very little upside to offering them $75,000. Sure, you may save some money in the short term, but you are also going to be looking to replace them in 12–18 months' time when they realise they can get more elsewhere. Professionalism, honesty, integrity, and all of the other desired values go two ways. If you want it from your people, then you must also provide it to your people.

Benefits & Wellness

When discussing solutions to employee experience, engagement, performance, and retention a lot of focus is naturally given to salary. This makes sense because it is the most immediate way an employee is rewarded financially. After all, none of us are working for free. But if you want to build a great employee experience that enables high engagement and performance, it would be wise to focus less on the actual salary and more on the additional benefits your organisation provides. Ultimately, salary is salary. It might be a little higher or lower than your competitors, but unless you are paying double what your competitors are (and let's be honest, you are not), then it is not a differentiator. Employee benefits, along with how you approach employee wellness in general, are a key weapon in differentiating yourself from the competition. This is because salary is monetary, but the type of employee benefits and wellness policies you have will also help shape the culture.

High performing companies have long prioritized employee wellbeing. This is proven by numerous pieces of research which show that employee health directly influences workforce behaviour and performance. To put it simply, a healthy workforce is a productive workforce. The healthier someone is, the better the quality of the work, and naturally, things such as attendance also increase significantly when the workforce is healthy. So, it should come as no surprise that roughly 75% of high performing organisations measure employee wellbeing on a consistent basis, as well as employee engagement scores and other performance measures. However, just as with employee experience, engagement, inclusion and diversity, and many other essentials, many organisations' wellbeing programmes leave a lot to be desired.

The reason why most employee wellbeing programmes struggle is because there is a lack of understanding that they are a business essential, not a nice to have. This is obviously a common theme running through this book. But it is simple, employees that are well make more money for an organisation. It is, therefore, vital that as part of the management capability training, there is a chapter on the organisations' benefit programmes and wellness policies. As with pretty much everything in an organisation, its success is dependent on management being educated on its importance. The key messaging is as follows, output and input are not the same thing. For example, do you want a salesperson who makes 100 phone calls a day or one that beats their sales target every year? You, of course, want one that delivers results, but most organisations focus on the input and not the output. The same is true when it comes to employee wellbeing and employee benefits.

A key differentiator between high and low performing organisations is whether they prioritise input (more activity) over output (actual results). High performing organisations almost always prioritise productive outcomes over high volume inputs. After all, the nature of being a high performer means that you produce better results from the same or less effort as others. To win the 100 m race at the Olympics, you need to run it in the fastest time. You can't claim you won simply because you ran for longer than the other people. It doesn't matter how much effort you put in; it's the output that matters. Again, this is backed up by research. We are all aware of which countries have the largest economies in the world, but something fascinating happens when you analyse each economy on productivity as opposed to total size. Research from organisations such as OECD shows that when you look at productivity, the big economies are not so big. The most productive economies are those that actually work the least hours. When ranking countries on productivity per hour work, those near the top of the rankings are always European countries that average under 30 hours of work per week. Ireland, Luxembourg, Netherlands, Belgium, Norway, and so on populate the top 10 economies in the world when ranked via productivity. On the other hand, countries such as China and Japan (which are ranked number 2 and 3 in total size at the time of writing) that have cultures of working much longer hours don't even make the top 10. In fact, Japan doesn't even make the top 20, and China doesn't make the top 50! The US and UK, which also work longer hours than their European counterparts also rank much lower. The US falls out of the top 5 economies when ranked via productivity, and the UK falls out of the top 10 economies as well.

Working more hours does not lead to better business outcomes. In fact, it has been proven for decades that the more hours you work, the less productive you are. More activity doesn't lead to more results. It actually leads to poorer quality results. Do you know why? People are tired! If you want your people to perform well, make sure they are able to take time off and rest. It is that simple. If you are not looking after your employees and ensuring they are well rested and looked after, they are going to burn out. This is why annual leave is such an important employee benefit. Ideally, you should be giving your people at least one week of each quarter at the minimum to ensure they have time to recharge. This is why European countries provide 4 weeks annual leave as a minimum to ensure workers are able to get a break and recharge. High performing organisations also commonly offer their people more than 4 weeks of annual leave each year. Research also shows that high performing employees take more annual leave than low performers. They take more time off, which in turn allows them to perform to higher standards for longer.

Beyond annual leave, there are a number of other employee benefits and wellness programmes to help ensure a workforce is healthy and, therefore, happy and productive. It should be clear by now that if your employee is not well, then they are likely to take more time off due to sickness, are more lethargic at work, and are generally less productive. So, a smart organisation would realise that it makes sense to not just ensure it provides its people with medical coverage for when they get sick to help them recover. It would also provide them with the tools to improve their overall health. This is why organisations such as Google invest so much in things such as gym memberships, onsite fitness classes, healthy snacks, and so on. They do not just do this because it's cool and people like it. They do this because they understand that the healthier their people are, the better they are able to perform. However, to ensure your workforce are healthy and productive, you also have to think beyond just the programmes. Having medical insurance for staff is important as it naturally ensures they are able to receive medical treatment and recover. Likewise, having access to fitness classes and so on is helpful to ensure your people are fit. But successful programmes go beyond just tactical initiatives and aim to embed a culture of wellness within the organisation.

This is why policies around things such as sick leave are also so important. Many organisations promote cultures of presenteeism, and this also significantly harms productivity, especially when sick. It is important for organisations to understand that coming to work when sick is often less productive than taking time off sick. The most common cause for a person to be absent from work is personal illness. Research shows that roughly 34% of all reasons someone doesn't come in are because they are physically sick. This is why organisations aim to invest a lot in trying to prevent absence. However, what is often overlooked is that lost productivity is much worse when someone comes into the office while unwell. If someone has a bad cold or flu, if they take a couple of days off, they will recover quickly. However, by not taking time to recover, the sickness often lasts for a week and sometimes more as the body has less chance to recover. This then results in the employee being unproductive for a much longer period than if they just took a couple of days off. In addition to this, because a member of staff is coming into the office while sick, there is also a much greater chance of infecting another employee. This would then cause them to also be less productive while they recover. Quite simply, if someone is unwell, absenteeism should be preferred over presenteeism, and a workforce and management culture should be aligned to this.

This also means ensuring that you have the appropriate policies and programmes to ensure people are able to take sick leave when required.

The best businesses understand that they should not just be looking after their employee's health but also provide support for the health of their employee's families as well. This is a topic that can often lead to a contentious debate but think about this simply. Let's assume you have an employee who has a sick child. Do you think your employee is going to be productive if they have to worry about medical bills and healthcare for their child? Do you think their performance could be severely impacted if they have no idea how they can afford treatment for their kid? Is there a strong possibility they might have to consider leaving your organisation to get more money to try and cover those expenses or to have time to take care of them? This is why it is common for high performing organisations to extend employee benefits to the families of their employees. The best even go beyond health and contribute to things such as a child's education, and so on. The reason is simple; if their employee doesn't need to worry about family concerns, then they are able to focus on delivering exceptional results. So, in order to deliver a great employee experience and ensure your people are focused and productive even during difficult times, ensure your programmes and policies take account of a person's family and not just the employee themselves. This is obviously easier said than done for smaller organisations that may be more constrained financially. But there are other ways to make up for it.

One of the easiest ways to help your people balance the practicalities of life with working commitments is to ensure you have the right policies and culture for flexibility. This is one of the real reasons why staff have craved a flexible working environment for over a decade. Flexible working has obviously come more into focus since the global pandemic. But let's be clear that it was not because of the pandemic that people wanted to work flexibly. Research performed in the years prior to the pandemic consistently showed that almost 90% of staff wanted the ability to work flexibly. The reason for this is simple. Life happens to all of us. So, if you assume an employee has a sick child, provide flexibility during this time. You might not be able to pay for all the medical bills, but you can provide flexibility. If the employee needs to take annual leave to take their child for a hospital appointment, is the employee going to feel like their employer is a good one? Of course not.

By trusting your employees to balance their work and home life and still get the job done, you build incredible loyalty from your employees. It should not matter if they did 5 hours of work from 9–2, went home early, took their child to the hospital for an appointment, and then made the time up over the coming days and caught up on work. What should matter is that the work was still delivered, and the employee was also able to take care of their family matter. If you rigidly stick to set hours and force employees to take annual leave for things like doctors' appointments, you are going to create a culture of resentment. This will not lead to a great employee experience that delivers high engagement and a performance culture. In fact, it is this, more than anything else, that exemplifies why organisations that champion productive outcomes over hours worked outperform others. It also costs nothing to provide flexibility. It is a policy that is free to implement and use.

Chapter 8: Performance Management

The truth is that most staff overwhelmingly detest the performance management cycle. In fact, the year-end performance review process has been found to consistently be one of the most disengaging experiences for staff. Quite simply, it is a horrendous employee experience. Gallup research showed that only 14% of staff feel motivated to perform better after their performance review. There is a key reason for this. Most organisations are guessing when it comes to the year-end review process. As we have discussed throughout this book, basic things such as proper SMART goals are rarely in place, which means that, in most cases, the year-end performance review process is incredibly subjective. This is why managers and HR professionals struggle to assess employees. They see their people turn up on time, attend the relevant meeting and send the required reports, so they assume they must be doing a good job. If that same person always seems to be working late, then surely, they are a great performer as they are working so hard! This is, of course, a lot easier than objectively measuring the performance of a member of staff based on quantifiable outcomes. These managers and HR professionals also often fail to realise that logically the person who is going home at 5 pm every day and also getting all of their reports done must surely be a lot more efficient and therefore a better performer than the person who had to work late every night to deliver the same output!

It is also important to understand that the manager's viewpoint of their staff is often a minority viewpoint. This causes a lot of issues because most organisations simply rely on the manager to tell them whether or not their team members have been performing. But they will only ever see a small percentage of what their team do. If they have a team of 4, in reality, they probably aren't even seeing 20% of what each of their team do. After all, it is impossible to see everything 4 people do. Simple maths means if they did nothing except spend time with their own team, watching what they did, then they would only see 25% of each of their team of 4. That is assuming they didn't have any work of their own to do or other meetings. This is why performance ratings increase by 14% on average if a performance review includes feedback from their peers. This, again, explains why performance reviews are one of the most disengaging parts of the employee life cycle. Can you imagine how you would feel if you were consistently being marked down by 14% simply because your boss didn't see some of the things you did? That is how most staff feel most of the time, and it is a blind spot all organisations should look to address, especially as it is so easy to get feedback from the rest of the team.

There is a sure-fire way to make the year-end performance process easy—set proper goals. Ultimately, a person's performance objectives for the year are what you are supposed to be assessing their performance against. So, it all starts with the goals you set at the start of the year or the start of their tenure with the company if they happen to be a new hire. You should then track these throughout the year, and when you get to the year-end review, a ten-year-old should be able to perform the performance assessment and get it accurate. It should be that obvious as to whether a member of staff has failed to achieve their objectives, met their objectives, or gone way above and beyond them. This should also theoretically translate to identifying who your low, middle, and high performers are for the year. What you will also find if you have set the right performance objectives for the year is that your employees will also accurately assess their own performance. Managers and HR often find they have to give their staff a reality check at year-end because they all think they are high performers for simply turning up for work and completing basic tasks. The reason for this is the same as to why staff are not happy with their year-end appraisal—proper objectives weren't set, and they haven't had clear communication. So, they assume they are doing amazing because they have no evidence to show them otherwise. By ensuring that proper goals were set, your year-end review process should become a lot easier. Your employees should self-assess accurately, and it should be self-evident as to who has and hasn't performed. Even if there isn't an accurate self-assessment, the goals should be so objective that it is impossible for anyone to misinterpret whether or not they have been achieved.

In addition to this, it is also important to ensure managers sit down and have a specific performance conversation with staff at least once a quarter and ideally at least once a month. This differs from the real-time day-to-day discussions they should be having with the team. As we have discussed, constant real-time feedback is critical, but it often centres around day-to-day challenges. So, it is important to carve out a separate time to link all of the day-to-day items back to the big performance objectives for the year.

209

This allows staff to understand not just the informal feedback they are getting but also allows them to understand how they are tracking against the full-year performance objectives that will define their end-of-year bonus, promotion, and pay review decisions. It should come as no surprise that staff who have regular performance check-ins perform better than those who do not. Despite this, roughly half of all employees do not have a performance conversation with their manager at least once a quarter. This also plays a significant part in why many members of staff react badly at year-end. If you have regular performance check-ins, you can compensate to a degree for having vague performance objectives. But if you are not setting proper goals and you aren't discussing performance regularly, it can be no surprise why more than 80% of staff find performance reviews a disengaging experience. These regular check-ins also allow managers and HR to pivot and fairly assess performance. For example, maybe a project was not delivered because IT was in the process of changing a core IT system, which means the project the member of staff was tasked with completing this year had to be delayed by 9 months. It would obviously be foolish to mark the member of staff down as having failed to meet expectations because of something like this. It would therefore allow you to understand everything well in advance and then push that performance objective to the next year and replace it with something else for this year. This is only possible with regular performance check-ins.

Also, remember that when assessing performance, you are supposed to be assessing the performance of a specific member of staff against their agreed-upon goals. In theory, this means that every single member of the team could exceed expectations. A common mistake managers and HR make is to mark down someone who exceeded expectations because someone else also exceeded expectations. There is no faster way to create resentment and disengagement in the team. If someone delivered 3 more projects than expected and another person delivered 4 more projects than expected, they both exceeded expectations. If you tell the person who delivered 3 extra projects you can only grade them as met expectations because someone else delivered 4, then you had better start looking to replace that member of staff. The question they will be asking in their heads, if not speaking directly, is *why did I bother to do all of that extra work when there was no benefit to it?* As an organisation that is trying to build a high performing environment to deliver great results, the last thing you want to do is disincentivise staff for going above and beyond the call of duty.

Retaining Your High Performers

It is, of course, impossible to discuss performance management without covering the topic of high performers. It's long been proven that high performers are more productive and efficient than their peers and essential to the bottom line of a company. They are critical to a company's long-term success. An organisation is only as good as the people working for the company, and without good employees, no company will succeed over the long term. Therefore, an organisation must retain its high performers. Yet managers and HR generally do a poor job at retaining their high performers. It is a fact that high performers have lower tenures on average than other members of staff, which has consistently led to the age-old question—how exactly do you keep them?

The starting point to retaining your high performers is to identify who your high performers are. This may seem obvious, but the truth is that many HR professionals and managers mistake their high performers for disruptive members of staff and their average performers for their high performers. This is at the core of why organisations struggle to retain their true high performers. High performers have lower tenures with organisations for a dual reason. The first is that they naturally achieve things faster than others and therefore get bored more quickly. But secondly, because management and HR often consider them disruptive, they then fail to provide them with suitable additional challenges, which leads to them deciding to go elsewhere for a new challenge. So, let me be clear, the members of staff who do exactly what is asked of them and complete all tasks on time with no issues are not your high performers. They are your average members of staff. A member of staff is hired to execute the tasks they are given, and if a member of staff is doing this, it's what they have been hired to do. This is the definition of someone who 'meets expectations'. A member of staff who doesn't deliver on the required tasks is 'failing to meet expectations'. Your high performers are the ones who 'exceed expectations'.

What this means is that your high performers are the ones doing additional things they have not been asked to do. This is why they are often tagged as being disruptive. They are going off script and getting involved in things their boss has not asked them to look at and so they can often be seen as loose cannons, always opening another can of worms. This is usually one of the easiest ways to identify a high performer because they often can't turn off the part of their brain that says, 'Oh, we should also fix this or change that'. They will rarely stop doing whatever task has been asked of them. In fact, they will often seek out additional projects and opportunities to grow. Expect them to be working on lots of random things in addition to their day-to-day duties. Another clear sign they are a high performer is that they always do this proactively; they don't sit around and ask for your permission. This, again, is why many can mistake them for troublemakers.

I knew one high performer who once left their manager stunned when they presented a proposal to replace their entire tech system. The whole team complained about the system, so they researched all the alternatives, performed demos, got quotes, etc. The manager was furious because he felt it was a waste of time and it wasn't the team's job to make suggestions on how to improve the system. Shortly after, the manager tried to put the member of staff on a disciplinary process. Fortunately, we actually replaced the manager with that team member instead! Unfortunately, the stats show that this doesn't happen enough, and instead, the high performer would be side-lined and eventually quit or get managed out in such circumstances. But if you have such an employee, make no mistake, they are a high performer. This is assuming, of course, they are also delivering in their day job. If they have completely neglected their primary responsibilities, then they are not meeting expectations. But if they have delivered their objectives and still find time to proactively do this, they are definitely a high performing member of staff you want to keep.

Once you have identified your high performer, the next step is understanding what motivates and drives them. This is obviously something you should do for all staff, but for high performers, it's even more vital. This is because pretty much all high performers are self-motivated and goal oriented. The reason they are putting in all of the extra efforts is because they are striving to achieve something bigger. There will be an underlying motivation. It could be something as simple as a promotion and/or a pay rise. It might be praise and recognition or a passion to drive change or operate autonomously—among many other motivating factors. But, one thing is for sure, a high performer will almost always have a clear picture of what they are working towards. So, by listening and understanding what drives them and tailoring your approach and interactions accordingly, you should then provide them with opportunities to learn/grow/develop in that direction. If you do not do this, then they are not going to stick around for the long term. They have no reason to. Others may stick around for job security, but a high performer knows there are plenty of other organisations out there who would be willing to hire them. So, you should build off their motivations and ensure you paint them a very clear picture as to how working for you will help lead them to where they want to go. This is a constant ongoing dialogue you need to have with them; it is not something you can mention once or twice over the course of a year. Most staff are happy to go with the flow, but high performers are wired differently.

Research has shown that for high performers, boredom is more likely to lead to disengagement and attrition than too much work. This is because high performers thrive on being challenged and having the next problem to solve. It is common for managers and organisations to want to slow high performers down. If a high performer can do something in 4 months, they are going to become frustrated if it takes 12 months. But corporate culture is full of excuses to slow down and not move so quickly. Phrases like 'let's not boil the ocean' are commonplace in the corporate world, and they are also one of the reasons why high performers opt to go elsewhere. By slowing them down or trying to have them reduce their pace, they are going to switch off. If you force a high performer to put up with a broken process for another year, every time they deal with that process, it is going to frustrate them. High performers achieve a lot more in a shorter time frame than other members of staff, and they always need the next challenge. If you can't keep them challenged, they will essentially run out of things to do and look elsewhere.

You should also avoid putting a high performer with low performers. This is a tactic many organisations opt to use in the hope that it will cause the low performers to improve. It rarely works that way. Rather than increasing the performance of the poor performers, it usually just leads to the high performer becoming disengaged. If you put Cristiano Ronaldo in a lower league team, the lower league players will not start playing like champions. What happens instead is that the high performer gets frustrated because they feel like they are carrying the rest of the team, and they get annoyed that others are not meeting their standards. If you are a high performer, you want to win the equivalent of championships, so if you put someone like that in a team who has no desire to win championships, it isn't going to be the poor performers that leave, but it will be the high performer. So, if you have a true high performer in your team, you will have to make a hard choice. You either meet the standards of the person and bring in other high performers, or you will lose the high performer. They are not going to stay in an environment where underperformance is tolerated.

Promotions

Did you know that most employees feel a promotion is not fairly decided based on ability and performance? It is true. According to a World at Work study, 65% of employees have doubts that a promotion is based on a fair assessment. While I would like to believe that those numbers are somewhat inflated, after all, everyone wants a promotion and thinks they are above average. The findings are common. We have already discussed how organisations often mistake their average employees for their high performers because they simply deliver the tasks they are asked to do. This is compounded by a lack of clear goal setting and, therefore, objective performance assessment. In addition, a manager's view, as we have also discussed, is often a minority opinion due to them only seeing a small percentage of the work done by any specific team member. So, how is an organisation supposed to decide who should be promoted to the next level?

Well, the first thing to remember is that it is important that you keep your assessment objective and fact driven. Unfortunately, bias is a real thing, and unconscious bias is how it normally manifests. Research from McKinsey and Lean In found that for every 100 men promoted to a management role, only 72 women were. The situation seems to have been made worse during the coronavirus pandemic, with research from the same group showing that 3 times more men were promoted than women in that time. Similar research focused on ethnic minorities showed similar challenges in the number of individuals from those groups being promoted. So, as you look to determine who should be promoted, remember that it is the performance and capability of the individual that matters the most. It is human nature to gravitate towards those more like ourselves, and as wonderful as it would be to connect as well with everyone regardless of personality type, race, gender, and various other things, it is rarely the case. But their individual traits do not matter; it is simply a case of objectively answering whether or not they exceeded expectations and demonstrated they have the capability to operate at a higher level.

There may be an employee in the team who you or the manager really like; maybe you or they have drinks after work, or your kids go to the same school or some other sort of connection. That is irrelevant at the end of the year. If they have not achieved their goals, they have not met expectations. It is that simple. Likewise, you or the manager may just dislike someone on the team. Maybe they support a different sports team or political party, and you or the manager don't quite click with them. Again, it should not matter. HR and the manager only need to ask how they performed against their performance objectives. Which, as we have discussed in previous chapters, should also include things

217

such as alignment to culture and values and not just—did they sell 10% more than last year?

When deciding if they are worth promoting, remember that doing their job well should not be enough to get promoted. Performing their job well is exactly what the organisation hired them to do. So, by performing well, all they are doing is exactly what they were hired to do. So, why should they be rewarded for doing simply what they are paid to do? This is one of the worst reasons to promote someone, and yet it is also the most common reason for someone to be promoted. As I have said before, organisations often mistake their average performers for their high performers. Simply delivering what is asked is the definition of an average member of staff. This is why there are so many poor managers in the world, and as I outlined in the early parts of this book, just because someone is a good accountant or software developer who performs the tasks they are given, it doesn't mean they will make a good manager of a team of people doing those jobs. Capability to perform the current role well does not equate to capability to perform the next role well.

Instead, you should be looking for those who have exceeded their goals for the year. These members of staff are typically those who have not only done what has been asked of them but have also proactively taken on additional problems to be solved without being asked. One of the paradoxes of corporate performance appraisals is that these individuals are often regarded as being difficult. But your true high performers are going to spot issues and bring attention to them. This can be incredibly frustrating to a lot of leaders. After all, no one likes to be told the way they may have been doing something for the last few years is inefficient and can be improved upon—especially if the leader was the one who put that process in place. But a key sign of an employee that should be promoted to the next level is one that spots problems and solves them. Ultimately, that is what you want from those who climb the ladder within the organisation. You want to ensure that those who make their way up the ladder are those who will ensure they are constantly driving the organisation forward and making it better. Those who stick to the script and only do what is asked of them are not going to improve the organisation.

So, if you want to build a strong organisation, it is imperative that you reward those who have demonstrated a willingness to take on more responsibility proactively in order to help improve things. If they were able to succeed in doing so, they are definitely a future leader because to make a change of some sort, you will need to also demonstrate the type of soft skills that can translate into positive management capability. However, it is important to beware of those who deliver change by questionable methods, such as throwing someone else under the bus or politicking to get it resolved, as opposed to driving change in a positive way. When making this assessment, also make sure you are confident the person proactively solved the problem without being asked. There is a big difference between an order taker who will do what is asked and those who push the organisation forward. You do not want to build a team of order takers who simply wait to be told what to do. Those who you promote are going to be the organisation's future managers and leaders, and you do not want them to be order takers who will do what they are told. You want your future managers and leaders to proactively improve both their teams and the wider organisation.

In addition, ideally, you also want to ensure the person you are promoting has a mindset of continuous learning. I discussed the 'Peter Principle' in my book *The Manager Handbook*—the principle that everyone eventually reaches a level of incompetence within an organisation. Often, the reason for this is not because they lack the capability to grow further but because they do not invest in acquiring new knowledge—which leads to their eventual stagnation and decline. It is the equivalent of trying to compete at the World Cup or an Olympics but still training in the same way you did as a junior in school. Natural talent will only get you so far, and for some very talented folks, that talent will get them very far. But at some point, to continue to progress, they are going to need to up their game and acquire new skills and knowledge to be able to compete against higher quality competition.

One of the easiest ways to identify those individuals early is by how much time they spend investing in themselves. This doesn't mean they went to 4 training courses last year because the company sent them on these courses. It means they choose to spend their own time learning. Are they spending time doing online courses themselves? Have they signed up for some sort of professional or academic qualification with their own money in their spare time? Are they always reading a new non-fiction book and acquiring new knowledge? Do they listen to a podcast or watch a YouTube tutorial during their lunch break at their desk while everyone else heads out for a nice break? As the saying goes, not all readers are leaders, but all leaders are readers. So, if you have a member of staff who is not only exceeding expectations by delivering on their objectives plus proactively solving other problems and also clearly invested in their own growth and development, that is exactly the type of person you should be rewarding with a promotion and giving more responsibility to. They will take both their team and the organisation forward.

Pay Review

I have never met anyone in management or HR that enjoys discussing the annual pay review decisions with employees. I am sure there must be some out there somewhere, but honestly, I have never met one. As a manager or HR professional, it is possibly one of the most difficult discussions to have. This is often because the entire process of how pay reviews are calculated is unclear to most employees. In fact, a World at Work survey showed that only 13% of employers felt their employees understood the process. This lack of understanding and transparency leaves a manager or HR professional in a tough spot. How do you keep a member of staff happy and engaged at pay review if nearly 90% of them don't even understand how the decisions are made? This challenge is often compounded by the fact that most staff overrate their own contribution and worth. Further research from the same group shows that 67% of employees feel they are not paid fairly. This is, of course, impossible because most staff are average and paid an average salary. But, of course, they do not see themselves as average. There are similar results when you ask drivers to rate their own driving ability, as 76% of drivers consider themselves above average, which, of course, is a statistical impossibility. There is no way that 76% of people can be above average. In my book *The Employee Handbook,* I also share a story of an old client of mine who paid their people the best salaries in their industry. Despite this, every year when the employee engagement results were published, the majority of staff would complain they were not paid competitively. This mentality among staff the world over makes HR and managers' roles incredibly difficult during the pay review.

However, it is possible to make the year-end pay review period a really easy time for management and HR. But to do this, you must first understand why the pay review process exists in the first place. The simplest explanation is that the pay review process serves two purposes. The first is inflationary. If you are unfamiliar with the concept of inflation, the easiest way to think about it is how prices increase year on year. Perhaps a loaf of bread cost $1 ten years ago, and today it costs $2 in the shop. Every year the cost of everything goes up a little. So, if staff did not have their pay review, they then would actually be poorer year after year because if costs go up every year and their salary doesn't, then eventually they are going to have to quit and go elsewhere so they can afford the cost of living. So, businesses provide their staff with a salary increase every year to ensure their people are not poorer by staying with the organisation and therefore don't have to leave. For some reason, most organisations don't link their annual pay rise directly to the rate of inflation, but it is essentially why we have a pay review each year. It would also make everyone's life easier if they simply linked it to inflation and communicated it as such. The second reason we have a pay review each year is because some people will have the scope of their roles changed during the course of the year and therefore need to have their salaries adjusted to compensate for the fact they are now doing more and, therefore, should be paid more. These people usually fall into two categories. They are the individuals who have either been promoted formally to a larger role, or maybe they haven't been promoted, but they have taken on more scope without the need for promotion. The promotion pay rises are self-evident, but managers and HR often get the approach wrong with those who have had their scope expanded.

For example, maybe they are an accountant, and your organisation hired them to prepare the accounts for a subsidiary, and they have done so well that they now prepare the accounts for another subsidiary as well. This increase in scope may not warrant a formal promotion, but they have clearly increased the scope of their role, and so you need to provide them with a salary increment to reflect the fact that they are doing more. This should be an increase that is larger than the rate of inflation because they are deserving of more because they are doing more than you initially hired them for. Failure to do this is why many managers and HR are often surprised when a member of staff quits after receiving some sort of promotion or expansion in scope. The person isn't quitting because they are being asked to do more; they are quitting because they have not been compensated for doing more than they were hired to do. If I hire you to come and redecorate my dining room, and then you do such a good job that I ask you to also do the rest of the house, you are not going to do it for the same original price. Yet organisations consistently expect their employees to do the equivalent of this when the scope is expanded. Do not make this mistake with your employees. Likewise, if there is no reward for doing more, you are clearly sending a message to staff that there is no point in trying to deliver on their objectives or going above and beyond because there is no reward for doing so.

This level of understanding is the key to turning the year-end pay review conversations into easy conversations. As shown by the statistics, 87% of staff have no idea how their pay review is calculated. So, it should not be surprising that two-thirds of staff feel they aren't rewarded fairly. By transparently communicating to your employees consistently how performance goals link to pay review outcomes and how it all ties together, you solve the problem of nearly 90% of staff having no idea how the decisions are made. By overcommunicating and being completely transparent, there are no surprises. Staff will know that if they want an above-inflation pay rise, then they have to exceed expectations and demonstrate clearly that they are delivering more value than they were hired to deliver. So, your software developer may have done a great job coding software for a project. But if they were hired specifically to code software for that project, then they shouldn't expect to get anything other than an inflation-related pay rise at the end of the year. If, on the other hand, they also set up a training programme proactively to train other software developers in the team, and it helped all of them improve performance, then clearly, they should expect an above-inflation pay rise. This means the organisation must also set proper SMART goals for employees so that these decisions are completely transparent and objective. There can be no wiggle room for misinterpretation. Performance outcomes always begin with the goals that are set.

Once you have completed the annual performance review process, the next step is for you to communicate the outcomes to your employees. This is the part that most managers and HR dread. But if HR and management have clearly communicated throughout the year how employees are performing against their goals and they understand how the pay review decisions are made, it will hopefully be an easier discussion. Still, there is one other thing you can do to make the actual pay review discussion easier. Avoid using percentages. When it comes to discussing the specific pay increase, percentages always sound less impressive. There is a huge difference in perception from a member of staff between hearing 'your pay rise is 2%' and 'you are going to have an extra $200 at the end of each month'. While $200 would be the exact same as 2% in this example, it is just how the mind works. Two hundred is a larger number than 2, and by framing it as an extra $200 of pay each month, staff can picture what they would do with that extra money a lot better than working out what an extra 2% of their pay is.

Finally, it is important to keep the tone of the conversation as neutral, objective, and factual as possible. It should be a very short, matter-of-fact discussion. Start by outlining what the person's goals were last year, recap the agreed performance review outcomes, and link that to the increment that is being provided. Unless the member of staff exceeded expectations, they should not be expecting anything other than a small inflation-related pay rise. So, unless you failed to articulate clear goals at the start of the year or accurately assessed performance, or failed to communicate throughout the year how they were performing and how that would impact their performance review—this should not be a surprise to them. Those who did exceed expectations should also have no issues because they should be adequately rewarded with a bigger increment than the rest of the staff. So, the logic for the decision should be self-evident, and therefore you only need to keep the conversation brief and factual. With this being said, the statistics show that even if everything is factual, objective, and self-evident, there will be certain staff who will always feel like they should be worth more. This is another reason to keep the conversation short. If you try to inject emotion and enthusiasm into the discussion and convince them it is fair, they're not going to want to hear it. In addition, the more you try to justify why the number is what it is, all the staff are going to hear is you telling them you don't value them or think they are worth more. It is a conversation with very little upside and a hell of a lot of downside. So, remember to keep it short, factual, and objective, and if you have done your job right throughout the year with goal setting, performance discussions, and general communication, you will be fine, and there will be no issues with the majority of your staff.

Chapter 9: Enabling Remote Working

In the aftermath of COVID-19, it seems like almost every HR and management group in every organisation is now trying to work out what the 'new normal' looks like. HR and management groups around the world are trying to work out either how to get their people back into the office or, having accepted that this isn't going to happen, working out how to manage an organisation where most folks aren't all sat in the office together at the same time. But the truth is that the 'new normal', as everyone seems to be calling it in 2022, is a reality that was becoming more and more common even before the pandemic happened. Remote working has been on the rise for several years, and even if you go back to the late 1990s, there were nearly 4 million remote workers in the US alone. The fact that so many businesses were caught short is more of a statement about their inability to keep up with technology and ways of working that were roughly 20 years old by the time the pandemic hit than anything else. Skype was founded in 2004, and VPNs have been around for even longer, so there really should not have been this big panic around how people would communicate or work if they were not in the office.

In fact, one of the key reasons why so many organisations are struggling with a 'return to the office' (at the time of writing) is because the pandemic has proven what many staff in white-collar office jobs already knew. There was little reason for them to be sat at a specific desk for a specific number of hours surrounded by their peers in order for them to deliver the required results. Research performed in the years prior to the pandemic consistently showed that almost 90% of staff wanted the ability to work flexibly and remotely. Staff now feel post-pandemic that they have proved their point during 2020 and 2021, as the results spoke for themselves. Many organisations delivered great results during the pandemic, and most of them were in industries that didn't require their staff to be sat in a fixed location. Organisations such as airlines, hotels, and so on obviously suffered, but nearly three-quarters of Fortune 500 firms made a profit during 2021 despite lockdowns and recessions. Nearly half of all Fortune 500 firms also made more money in 2021 than they did the previous year. In 2020, which is obviously when the outbreak happened, and the world went into full lockdown, nearly 70% of Fortune 500 firms made more money than they did in 2019 when there was no pandemic. Research for the past 20 years has shown it is more productive to work remotely, and the business results of 2020 and 2021 proved it. During a period when business results were expected to be a disaster, most organisations actually achieved better results than before the pandemic!

Despite the overwhelming majority of staff (practically all staff) wanting to be given the flexibility to work remotely at least part of the time and the clear benefits to organisations who are able to enable their staff to work remotely, there is still a resistance among HR and management to embrace this. In fact, research showed that for every 1 member of staff that supports a return to the office full time, 3 members of management are eager to return to the office on a full-time basis. Embracing the ability to work flexibly has also been shown to provide organisations with a clear advantage in attracting and retaining talent. So, why are many in HR and management continuing to bury their heads in the sand and insist it isn't working? At its core, this can be summed up with the phrase: 'But, how do I know our employees are working?' which seems to be the common theme at the heart of those in HR and management that are struggling to adapt to managing those who are not physically in the office with them. This phrase is also a clear sign that the organisation was not assessing performance properly when the member of staff was in the office. Because ultimately, whether a person is physically sat in the office in front of you for 8 hours a day or you never physically see them, it should be incredibly self-evident whether or not they have produced the required results. A person being sat at a desk for specific hours does not mean they are working; it does not mean they are productive. The same principle applies to those that work late. A person's performance has nothing to do with their physical location at all; instead, it has everything to do with the output they produce. If you are relying on presenteeism to judge performance, then you are not assessing performance properly, regardless of whether a person is in the office or out of the office.

The truth is that this also isn't a new problem. While COVID-19 and the larger shift to remote working have impacted a significant percentage of the population, there are a couple of groups of managers and HR who had had to deal with this challenge long before anyone had ever heard of coronavirus. These were the organisations that had people who were managing international teams or teams who were working nationally or across multiple offices within one country. There are those who were promoted into these kinds of roles and thrived, and there are those who failed to get results. Those who thrived displayed the scalable traits of good employee experience and good people management outlined in this book and my management book *The Manager Handbook*. Those who failed did so because they were unable to let go of outdated approaches and ways of thinking. For example, a manager can compensate ever so slightly for having poor management capability if they are managing a small team by simply being a terrible micromanager who needs to see everything. But that behaviour is not scalable to larger teams. This is why organisations that enable democratic and laissez-faire management styles are significantly more successful than organisations that use autocratic styles. So, the very first step to enabling a remote team to succeed is to trust your people. Ultimately, your employees were hired because they displayed the relevant capabilities to perform their roles, and the reason they have not been fired as of yet is that, on the whole, they have been performing to an acceptable standard. So, why do you think the staff are going to magically turn into poor performers simply because they aren't sat at a desk in front of their manager? This is the definition of a lack of trust. So, if you can't trust your people to perform the job they were hired to do, you are not going to be able to build a successful organisation regardless of team size or location of your employees. The culture will always be toxic because, without trust, you can't build anything of substance.

Once your organisation has been able to clear this mental hurdle of being able to treat your employees like grown-ups who understand they have a job to do, the next step is to set clear performance objectives for them. If you want to know if your people are working or not, performance objectives are the clearest way to determine this. If a member of staff has to provide a report by Friday, there are going to generally be three different outcomes to this. The first is that the manager gets the report which means they were working. The second is going to be that they highlight challenges and ask for guidance and support, and they might miss the Friday deadline as a result, but again it is clear they are working. The third is that the manager doesn't hear from them, and they don't provide them with the report. At which point, whether they are working or not, they have failed to deliver. So, regardless of whether a member of staff is in the office or not, your ability to set clear performance objectives remains of paramount importance to determine whether or not your team are performing.

This approach is exactly the same whether or not they are in the office. It does not matter how many hours they worked on it or where they worked on it; all that matters is that the objective was met. Their ability to spend a specific number of hours working on it in one particular location is arbitrary at best. More importantly, if your member of staff is able to get an entire week's worth of deliverables completed by the end of the day on Monday, why would you force them to sit at a desk and be busy for the remaining four days? They are a clear high performer who should be praised and rewarded for such efficiency, not chastised for not spending enough time working on it sat at a desk. Who cares if they took a 4-hour lunch break every day if they have delivered all of their performance objectives? Do you employ them to work for a specific number of hours a day or to deliver a specific set of results? If you set proper objectives, then it should be clear whether or not your team are performing.

After setting clear performance goals, the next step is to establish a clear communication plan with management and employees— just as you should when working in the office. Of course, the challenge, as we have already outlined, is that many managers don't do this properly in the office and so fail to do this effectively with staff who are not in the office as well. Rather than relying on being able to just ask staff something at any time because they are in the office together, they should instead set up a formal communication cadence with their remote team (and their team in the office, for that matter) to discuss performance. As we have discussed in multiple chapters, real-time feedback, recognition, and coaching are essential elements of creating a great employee experience that delivers high levels of engagement and performance. So, ensure managers establish a pattern of communication with the team. This should consist of both formal meetings to discuss performance and deliverables and also informal channels of communication.

For example, they may have a weekly meeting with the team to go through key deliverables and ensure they have the chance to raise any issues with them at the start of the week. This allows the team to provide them with a quick update and ask for help if required. In addition, they would set up a formal monthly catch-up to discuss how things are progressing against their overall performance objectives. On top of this, perhaps a Slack channel or WhatsApp group is set up to enable the team to share information in real time, ask clarifying questions, and so on. By ensuring managers have a clear communication strategy with the team, they are able to ensure you remain on top of the key issues. But it is important not to slip into a micromanager here. If your team are spending 5% or more of their week just updating management (this is 2 hours based on a 40-hour week), it's likely they are smothering their team. Likewise, it doesn't take much effort to phone up a team member and provide some real-time recognition for a piece of work they have just completed. They don't need to be sat together in the office to be able to communicate.

So far, so good, right? Enabling a remote team should sound relatively straightforward so far. You have set clear performance objectives and established a set of checkpoints to ensure the team are on track and have the required support and guidance. But there is one topic that has really confounded HR and management in the shift to remote working, and it's one that has been the leading cause of people claiming people should come back to the office. This topic is building team culture and engagement. In the post-COVID-19 world, this seems to be the thing those who have resisted the shift to modern ways of working cling to the most. How do you build culture if the team are not in the same place? Again, the answer is that it is pretty much done the same way as you would in the office, but you just leverage digital tools to enable the same behaviours.

Before I outline some of these methods—let me ask you a question. In order to build and maintain a friendship, do you need to spend 40 hours a week sat next to your friend in the same physical location? Do you need to spend 40 hours sat in the same location with your spouse or kids to ensure a good relationship?

Do you need to spend 40 hours a week sat in the same location with your mother, father, cousin, or uncle to maintain a positive relationship? The answer, of course, is no. So, the idea that the only way you can build a productive working relationship with someone is by being sat in the same physical location as them all the time is complete nonsense. It is easy to build culture and rapport amongst a team, even if they are not sat in the same location, by doing exactly what you do with all of your other relationships. You take advantage of technology and maintain contact through those channels. I guarantee you are part of some sort of WhatsApp group (or similar App) with some friends or family, and you all share photos and updates of key events such as birthdays, photos of the kids, etc. What stops you from doing this for your employees?

It would take all of 2 minutes to set up a couple of channels for the team, and you could have one that is work-related and one that is culture-focused. You can encourage folks to share what TV shows they are watching, plans for the weekends, photos from holidays, and so on. This is exactly as they would do in the office anyway, but as they are now not in the office full time, they can just share it via the team chat. Managers and HR can also instigate and encourage such sharing. It doesn't take much to type out a message saying, 'Can anyone recommend a cool new show to watch?' or 'Any suggestions on where to take the kids this weekend?' In addition, HR or managers could block out everyone's diary for a weekly digital team lunch where they all just chit-chat on Microsoft Teams or Zoom for an hour instead of doing it in person. The same approach can be taken for team building activities. If you head over to Google and just search for virtual or digital team building activities or engagement activities, there are literally millions of results filled with suggestions and ideas. If it is someone's birthday, instead of giving them a card and cake in person, have it delivered to their house and arrange for the team to all sing Happy Birthday over a group video call. There are also tools such as Miro and Mural that allow you to run entire workshops digitally, complete with post-it notes and whiteboards, without ever needing to be in the same location.

We do so many of these things as standard in our personal lives, but for some reason, when it comes to our professional lives, there are still many who have failed to adapt. But you really are only limited by your imagination. It is incredibly easy to replicate the type of team bonding you would do in person via a digital alternative. Do not misunderstand me, though; I am not saying there is no reason to do any of these things in person. What I am saying is that there are plenty of ways to get the exact same results without requiring everyone to be present in person. Especially as the workforce has made its feelings clear, they would like to have the option to work flexibly. This means there is no reason to enforce an arbitrary rule that someone must be in the office for a specific number of hours a week. Hybrid working is undoubtedly the best possible option, but hybrid does not mean a fixed number of hours. If you force everyone to come into work on Tuesday, for example, they are going to resent you for it. There is no reason for them to come in except because you have said you want them to be there in person.

However, if you can provide your people with a reason they would want to come into the office, they will also look forward to coming in. For example, if it is someone's birthday next Tuesday, well, then why not suggest having everyone travel in for the day and you can have a nice team lunch and maybe some celebratory drinks after work? You will find most people on the team will be happy to come in. If you then suggest that because everyone is coming in, it could also be good to spend that morning having a team meeting to go through a couple of key projects and get everyone on the same page; again, everyone is going to think that makes sense. But if you just arbitrarily insist on them coming in for a fixed number of hours or days, then you are not going to build culture and engagement. You are instead going to build resentment and disengagement. If you get all of this right, then again, just as with being in the office, it should be relatively straightforward. Your employees will have clear deliverables, clear communication, and a good team dynamic. Performance assessment will also remain simple because they will either deliver their objectives or they won't. So, they will either meet expectations, fail to meet expectations, or exceed expectations, and it really wouldn't matter if they were there physically in person or not. The truth is that it shouldn't matter where they are based or what hours they work. All that should matter is whether or not the results were delivered, and you don't need everyone to be in the same location to manage that.

Chapter 10: Leaver Experience

The most overlooked element of employee experience is what is known as leaver experience. The truth is that most organisations pay a hell of a lot of attention to those who are joining the organisation but very little to those who are leaving the organisation. This is often a huge mistake for two reasons. The first is that those who are not leaving will be watching how you treat people when they do leave, and if it isn't great, it is going to lead to them feeling like your organisation doesn't actually value or respect its people. The second is that your entire employer brand is dependent on what your own people say about you, and if you treat them like crap on the way out, well, your brand isn't going to be good. As Maya Angelou once said, people will forget what you did, but they will never forget how you made them feel. So, you could have the best policies and management in the world, but if the second someone quits, you discard them and leave them feeling unappreciated, well, your brand is going to suck.

A lot of the challenges organisations now face with this issue have their roots in the 1980s. Prior to this period, prevailing economic theories were about long-term benefits for all within an organisation. If a company was making $1 billion a year, then everyone was happy. Employees were happy because they had long-term job security. Management was happy because the business was successful. Shareholders were happy because their business paid them a nice dividend every year. Then this all changed and led to a shift in increasing value for shareholders as

237

the primary goal of most businesses. So, organisations then had to find ways to make more money each year. This led to organisations beginning to downsize departments and letting people go to increase profits. So, rather than making $1 billion, they let a few thousand workers go, and then they could give their shareholders $1.1 billion instead. It is this shift in priorities that led to a decline in the average tenure of employees. This shift also led to significant erosion of the loyalty employees give to their employers. After all, if their organisation won't think twice about shutting down their division to bump the share price by a couple of percentage points, why would they be loyal to the company? It isn't like the company is losing money. The company is doing fine and making a decent profit.

The impact of this shift has led to what is known as 'survivor syndrome' within organisations. It shows that employees that stay with organisations become significantly less productive because of how those who left were treated. Research has shown that 74% of employees who remained felt they became less productive after seeing colleagues leave under negative circumstances. A further 69% say the organisation's product and services also declined as a result. In addition, 87% say they wouldn't recommend the organisation as a place to work. Furthermore, 64% say the work of their colleagues also declined, and 81% also add that customer service levels also fell as a result of seeing people leave the organisation in a negative situation. On top of all of this, 77% of those who stayed with the organisation reported an increase in errors and mistakes, and 61% also said they had a negative view on the organisation's future prospects. All of this is just from the people who stayed with the organisation and saw others leave in negative circumstances. This is why it is so important to also pay attention to leaver experience. If you don't look after those who are leaving the organisation, well, your employees are not going to see that as a good sign of things to come for them.

Dealing with Leavers

So, what should you do when an employee leaves? Well, the starting point should usually be to congratulate them. Unless you are a horrible organisation that has been treating your people so badly that they would rather quit than continue working for you, it is highly likely that the reason one of your employees has resigned is because they have secured an excellent new opportunity. When there is a resignation, HR or a manager's natural response is to look at the scenario in one of two ways. The first response is for them to look at it from a purely selfish perspective. This means how the resignation impacts them and the team. While this is a perfectly natural instinct, it sends a really negative message to the rest of the team. This is because none of your employees are thinking they want to do the same job in your company for the rest of their careers. They will all desire to try new things and look to grow and develop in some shape or form. If they see your organisation react negatively to one of the team taking a positive step forward in their career, they are highly unlikely to think you care about them and their career prospects. The second approach involves them putting aside their own ego and being proud that a member of your organisation has secured an amazing new opportunity. This type of organisation understands they likely played a key role in helping them to develop the required capability to secure that new opportunity. They could have joined the company 3 years ago and knew very little. The organisation invested time in helping them grow, develop, and succeed, and now they are able to take the next step and move on to something even bigger. They could not have achieved this without the support of the organisation, and the organisation is proud of what they have achieved. This type of organisation understands that attrition is normal and, in this day and age, if you can get three good years out of an employee, then it is a great win for both you and them. The employee's response in this scenario is actually to become more engaged and work harder. They understand they are working for an organisation that is willing to help them develop their own careers and make sure they support the organisation's objectives in return.

With this being said, not all leavers are voluntary leavers. It is an unfortunate reality of the business world that some people (most people, actually) are going to be let go at some point. Research shows that about 40% of all employees will get fired at least once in their career. On top of this, they are also likely to be the victim of an organisation downsizing or restructuring several times throughout their career. In this case, it is obviously very hard to celebrate the new opportunity. But it is very easy to support these people in their transition. The organisation should ensure they have an offboarding programme for involuntary leavers. This should include things such as helping the leavers to update their CV, get introductions to external recruiters, industry bodies, and other organisations to help them with their job search, and so on. This doesn't need to be overly complex; most organisation's internal talent acquisition teams will be able to help set something up pretty easily. They will already have relationships with various recruiters, job boards, industry bodies, and so on. They could also run workshops themselves for the leavers on things such as updating CVs, searching for new opportunities, and improving interview skills. If the team don't have the capacity to do this, it should not be hard to find a third party who can do the same thing.

Communicating the News

Once you have finished either congratulating the employee on securing a great new opportunity or explaining they are going to have to leave, but you will support them through that journey, the next step is for you to tell the wider organisation. Many organisations make the mistake of trying to keep the fact someone is leaving a secret, but this logic is flawed. There is no easier way to lose the trust of your employees than to be seen as hiding something from them because here is a secret for you; at least one person in the company probably knew the person was going to leave before you did. Team members become close, and they talk. As we have discussed, employees move on. It's a fact of life, and if your employees see you are hiding something as trivial as an employee accepting another offer to work elsewhere, or worse, that you are letting someone go against their will, they will begin to wonder what else you are hiding from them. No company can be successful if there is not openness and transparency.

In addition to losing the trust of employees, this lack of transparency also prevents an effective handover from taking place. Quite simply, the more notice people have that someone is going to leave, the smoother the transition will be. In many organisations people only find out someone is leaving when they receive an email saying it is someone's last day. This doesn't leave enough time to ensure that knowledge is shared adequately so that results can still be delivered. Also, by not sharing that the person is leaving, you place a huge amount of pressure on the member of staff that is leaving. For example, it is very common that they end up in meetings discussing projects due in 3 months' time while knowing full well they are not going to be there to deliver the project. This means you are essentially forcing them to lie to their colleagues. None of this creates a great experience for anyone.

It is also important to maintain a positive vibe while communicating with others and throughout the notice period of the staff member who is leaving. No business likes to lose employees. A lot is written about high performer retention, and I have gone into detail on this topic in previous chapters, but even average performing employees contribute a lot to the organisation over time. They may not be rockstars, but that does not mean they do not have value. They become friends with their co-workers, help with a lot of the small things, and are a critical part of the overall ecosystem. They may not be revolutionising the industry, but they are keeping things ticking over, and this is often underrated. Very few people thought of food delivery workers as essential staff or high performers, and then the COVID-19 pandemic hit, and suddenly, it dawned on everyone just how critical they were to the ecosystem. This person may be leaving, and maybe they were even a poor performer, but if they always brought in cookies for the team on a Monday morning, having baked them over the weekend, they are going to be well liked and missed by the team. It is human nature. If you work with someone every day for a few years, they are going to be missed when they leave. So, it is important that you are not negative about them. If your employees see management or HR speaking negatively about team members, they will assume you are doing the same about them. This won't lead to a healthy work environment that leads to high engagement and high performance.

Valuing Their Contribution

There is an additional element to leaver experience that is consistent throughout the entire employee lifecycle—recognition. This is because unless you hired some sort of psychopath who you had to fire after a couple of weeks for gross misconduct, an employee would have contributed to the organisation. Recognising this allows for all parties to get closure and feel good about the breakup. Because when an employee leaves an organisation, that is what it is. It is a professional breakup. The employee, co-workers, and employer all depended on one another for a number of years. There were good times and bad times, great successes, and projects gone wrong. Then one day, that's it. Those relationships are finished. The employee and a co-worker might have had lunch together every day for 5 years, and now, all of a sudden, they are gone. A manager might have gone to that same employee every time they needed someone to save a failing project. The employer might have relied on that employee to also lead one of the social groups within the organisation. Maybe they were the person who had led and organised the dads at work group or the women in tech group. With one decision, all of that no longer exists, and it affects many within the organisation. So, it is vital to ensure that the organisation is seen to value the contribution of the person. The employee feels they were valued for the time with the company and co-workers can also say goodbye and share their appreciation.

There are, of course, many ways to do this both formally and informally. But, as with many elements of organisational culture, it is easier to achieve the desired outcomes by ensuring there is a consistent approach across the organisation. Failure to do this is why there is rarely any sort of consistent employee experience within the organisation. As we have discussed elsewhere in this book, managers, when left to their own devices, will do what they feel is right. Unfortunately, they aren't all going to act in the same way. Some people will handle the leaver experience terribly, and others will handle it well. The same is true of all other elements of employee experience. It is true in goal setting, performance assessments, culture and team building, mentoring, coaching, employee development, etc. So, it is usually helpful to put a few policies in place to ensure there is a baseline of accepted norms across the organisation.

The starting point does not need to be overly complex. For example, the organisation could start by ensuring that all employees who leave receive a leaving card signed by people across the organisation. It really doesn't take much effort or cost much to implement this. HR could even ensure that they bulk order cards at the start of each year so that no one needs to worry about going out to get one. Then all of the managers, team members, and wider peers of the employee who is leaving can sign the card and share stories, memories, and other messages. Perhaps the message is a memory of a project that was worked on, maybe a funny story from a team bonding event, or maybe something more personal, as they have also become friends outside of the office. In addition to talking about the memories, the employee should also be congratulated on securing a new role and/or wished luck for the future if they are leaving involuntarily.

In addition to providing the leaver with a card, there should also be a more formal email sent to the wider team or organisation acknowledging the contribution of all leavers. This is done for two reasons. The first is that it will allow the leaver to feel appreciated, but it also has the added benefit of showing the wider employee group that the organisation values its people. Depending on the size of the organisation, it may not be possible to do this across the whole organisation for each leaver. It might instead be more appropriate to be done within their relevant department instead, but make no mistake, it should be done. The official email, which should be sent out by the relevant senior leader, should document all of the contributions the employee has made while being with the company. This should be an extensive email listing all of the work the employee has done during their tenure. Business as usual activities, extra projects, feedback from peers and managers to really highlight what the employee did and how that brought value. It will send a clear message to all that the organisation believes in the value of its people and the contributions they make.

To top it all off, it should be standard practice to arrange a time to allow everyone to get to say their goodbyes to the employee that is leaving. This can be done in a variety of different ways. It might be as simple as arranging a team lunch or as extravagant as arranging a full-blown leaving party in a bar near the office after work. If budget is an issue, then it could be as simple as getting everyone on a Zoom call for 30 minutes or having everyone come over to the desk in the office at a specific time. Regardless of the method (and cost), the aim should be the same. It provides everyone with an opportunity to say goodbye, say thank you, share memories, and so on. You should also aim to get at least their direct manager, and ideally also some other senior people to say a few words to acknowledge some of the work that has been done by the individual. This all has the benefit of also opening the door for a return down the line. Even if they don't come back, former employees are proven to be a great source of referrals for both new hires and new business. So, it always makes sense to ensure they leave with a sense of recognition and respect. There are, of course, a number of other things that can be done to really go above and beyond for leavers, including gifts and personalised videos from the CEO, among many other things. But at a bare minimum, there is very little excuse for not providing your leavers with a card, email, and some sort of formal goodbye event. It hardly requires any budget and provides significant benefits to both the leaver and those staying.

Having said all of this, it is important to remember that the leaver process is not just about cards and leaving parties. Do you think the leaver or your remaining employees are going to react well to the organisation screwing someone out of a $50,000 bonus because you gave them a card and a leaving lunch? It is incredibly important to also ensure the organisation acts ethically in its conduct during the leaving process. This might seem obvious, but the truth is there are literally millions of horror stories relating to people leaving organisations. These stories relate to all types of individuals. It could be that the hiring manager gives an awful reference to try and sabotage their move elsewhere. There are countless stories of HR bending policy rules to ensure an employee does not get paid all they are entitled to. Even CEOs who have fired employees just so they can say the employee did not resign. This is not how you run a professional business, and not only does it create an awful experience for the leaver, but other employees see this and then think they need to also leave quickly as their company is run by terrible human beings. I don't doubt that you would ever do something so disdainfully unethical, but it does happen, and sometimes even in very well-regarded companies. So, ensure that there are clear policies and procedures around what people are entitled to when leaving and make sure these are transparently shared and widely available. There is no better way to create mass disengagement among your workforce than for their organisation to behave unethically.

Exit Interviews

Do you want to know a great way to improve employee experience and prevent talent from leaving? Here is a crazy idea:

how about asking the talent that is leaving why they are leaving and using this information to improve the current environment? This is obviously known as an exit interview, but it is criminally underused by organisations. The whole reason an exit interview existed in the first place was to understand why people were leaving so that an organisation could proactively take steps to then improve the company. But at some point, this purpose has been diluted, and in many workplaces, it is now just seen as another process or task that has to be completed, as opposed to a powerful listening tool that allows an organisation to become stronger. This leads to organisations failing to address the issues, and they then get worse over time, and more and more employees don't even bother sharing their opinions as they don't see it as a worthwhile exercise.

This approach and the problems that it causes are, of course, practically identical to the issues surrounding employee engagement surveys. The whole point of the mechanism is to allow for employees to highlight what is and is not going well. The organisation is then supposed to act on this information to ensure the organisation becomes stronger. In addition, there is an argument to be made for an organisation to conduct stay interviews as opposed to exit interviews. By the time an exit interview is conducted, it is usually too late. It is not going to stop a great talent from walking away. They have already decided to go. It is why you are discussing their exit with them. A more proactive strategy, which can be tied into the performance conversations that should be had each month, is to get ahead of the issues. The aim is to discuss what employees would want to see more of in order for them to stay over the long term. This would then theoretically remove the need for exit interviews to be had outside of a small percentage of people who still move. There is obviously a big difference between someone leaving because their boss sucked, or they aren't being provided with growth opportunities and a person leaving because they are a superstar who has been offered a double-your-money deal to jump to a competitor.

The only way to get these kinds of insights is to ensure that exit interviews are consistently conducted so that your organisation can collate meaningful insights allowing you to make informed decisions. For example, I once had a client who promoted an employee into a first-time management role. They were given the opportunity to manage a department of 17 employees. Within 12 months, this new manager only had 8 employees left within their department. There had been a mass exodus, and in the exit interview, every single one of the employees told the exact same story. The manager who was promoted into his first management role had pretty much no management skills. He could not communicate any plans, vision, or strategy, never showed any appreciation to team members, and insisted on micromanaging everything. This led to two key insights. The first was that the organisation had clearly promoted someone into a management role who was ill-equipped for it. The second was that this was a familiar trend in the organisation across departments and countries. They realised they were promoting people based on their technical expertise in the last job and not because they had the capability to perform the next job, which required a different skill set, specifically management skills. They made significant changes to their promotion criteria and developed a new management training programme to ensure those either in management or moving into management had a baseline of capability to succeed. The result of this was that within 2 years, their employee attrition rate had gone from 28% to 6%, and they delivered their most profitable business results ever.

With this being said, it is important to ensure that feedback is contextual. The example I have just shared is one that clearly demonstrates a clear issue that needs to be resolved. However, not all feedback from exit interviews is as clear-cut. Ultimately, the reason someone is leaving is more than likely because they feel they aren't getting treated in the way they want in your organisation. But just because someone is unhappy, this doesn't necessarily mean there is a problem. For example, you could have a manager who has a team of 20, and in 4 years of managing them, they consistently have engagement scores over 90% and an attrition rate of 5%. It is possible that one of the 5% stated in an exit interview that the manager is a terrible tyrant who treats their people terribly. The chances of this being accurate are very low. Sure, this person might potentially be a terrible person, but you have to look at the information in totality. One person saying this in 4 years, while the rest of the team happily stay where they are and praise the environment, doesn't match up. Therefore, the amount of investigation that should be done is a lot lower than in the first example. The problem, of course, is that in many organisations exit interview feedback is more like the first example, and the organisation does nothing. If you have more than half the team quit in a year, and they were all saying the same thing, it shouldn't matter who the manager is. Something clearly needs to be done.

Let me also be clear, if there is consistent attrition in a team, then that is a clear sign of poor management capability. People don't leave companies, they leave managers. So, if you have a team experiencing consistent attrition over a period of a few years, I can almost guarantee that the manager is the problem. However, it can be difficult to prove this with data. This is because not everyone is going to be open about their reasons for leaving. They worry that if they are too honest, it might jeopardise their reference, or they might just not want to say anything too critical. Additionally, as we discussed in the design thinking section of this book, sometimes asking a different question will provide you with different answers. If you ask someone why they are leaving, well, they are leaving because someone else offered them a better opportunity. However, if you asked them why they decided to start looking elsewhere, they will soon begin to tell you how they resented being passed over for a promotion, or that they didn't get any recognition for a specific project they delivered, etc.

These nuances can sometimes make it difficult for HR teams to get enough information to make an informed decision as to whether or not they need to act. After all, if a manager is having 50% attrition each year, but no one is blaming the manager in the exit interviews, what can you do? The answer to this is to use multiple methods to conduct exit interviews. Different people will respond differently via different channels and at different stages in their exit. For example, someone is really unlikely to throw their boss under the bus if they have to then serve 3 months' notice under them, get a good reference for their new employer and ensure they get paid all the bonuses they are owed. But if you were to ask them 3 months after they left the organisation once they had joined the other company, they are a lot more likely to be open and candid. They then have nothing to lose anymore.

The method can also influence proceedings in multiple ways. If you are losing a high performer, ideally, you would love that person to come back someday. So, ensuring you conduct a high-touch face-to-face exit interview, you increase the possibility of maintaining some sort of rapport with the high performer. If you were to then stretch out the exit interview over a few months, this would also allow you to build a bridge to show that you valued their opinion, acted on feedback, and also leave the door open for them to change their mind. After all, about one-third of new hires realise they have made a mistake when moving in the first few months of a new position. For other employees, research has shown that when you remove the face-to-face component of an exit interview, people are more likely to open up. Most people find it difficult to provide negative feedback to friends, so it's even harder to do so in a professional setting to someone in a formal position of authority. So, conducting the exit interview over the telephone or via some sort of instant messaging chat or online survey can also help to ensure you receive more candid responses that will help you to identify root cause issues.

Beyond the Organisation

There is one final key differentiator between high performing organisations and the rest of the field in how they look at employee experience. This differentiator is that they do not only aim to treat their existing employees well—regardless of whether they have just joined or are planning to leave—but they also prioritise their former employees as well. You read that right. The best employee experiences do not only apply to a person's time with an organisation, but they also actually extend far beyond their tenure with the company. Now, before you start rolling your eyes and saying that the organisation barely has time to look after its existing employees, hear me out. Just as with employee experience, employee engagement, and many other so-called fluffy topics, the truth is that looking after your former employees is actually beneficial to the bottom line of your organisation. Some of the best companies in the world have had this figured out for a while, which is why they invest so heavily in alumni networks to maintain positive ties with their former employees. This is because former employees are proven to be a great source of referrals for both new business and new employees.

The research on this is extensive, but what is interesting about the research conducted on looking after former employees is that some of the best research has actually been conducted by businesses themselves. One of the best examples of this is Microsoft. Microsoft is obviously one of the most iconic and successful organisations of the past generation; it is very hard to imagine a world without them. At the time of writing, they also have in excess of 200,000 employees, which means they have a significant number of former employees they are able to analyse. What they found many years ago was that employees who feel appreciated and leave an organisation on good terms will not only remain fans of the brand, but they will actually continue to both use its products and recommend its products to others.

These findings were part of the catalyst for Microsoft deciding to build a huge global alumni network that spans over 50 countries and tens of thousands of employees.

When Deloitte analysed its own group of former employees, it led to similar findings, which is why Deloitte's own alumni network has several hundred thousand members globally. As Deloitte worked through the journeys of those who left the organisation, they realised that most of their employees weren't actually going to competitors; they were going to potential clients. It also became incredibly obvious that those former employees who had a positive experience with the organisation were much more likely to provide business opportunities to Deloitte than those that had a negative experience. It was, therefore, a no-brainer for Deloitte to not just ensure that as many people as possible left on good terms but that they maintained a positive relationship with the brand even after leaving. This is why Deloitte regularly hosts alumni events, sends communications to former employees about the organisation, and so on. Deloitte has also reaped a second benefit from maintaining strong relationships with its alumni. They find it a lot easier to hire great talent than some of their competitors who don't invest as much into their alumni infrastructure. Deloitte sees, on average, about 3,000 former employees return to the organisation each year. In addition, they see several thousand more hired by Deloitte via referrals from their alumni network. Many organisations struggle to attract enough talent. Now imagine being able to ask several hundred thousand people for a referral at any moment? This is why it's so important to ensure your employee experience also extends to those who are no longer with the organisation.

To build a successful alumni network, it is important to approach the concept strategically end to end rather than aiming to build one via a sporadic set of tactical activities. The approach is actually very similar to the method of building a successful talent community which I outline in my book *The Talent Acquisition Handbook: A Practical Guide to Candidate Experience.* This method is to first segment all of the individuals as part of the alumni group and build personas around them. So, you might have groups such as business leaders, technology, or other technical experts, and so on. Then you curate specific content and events to keep them plugged into what is happening within the organisation. For example, you might send a note to all former employees each quarter sharing the latest business results or other important and comprehensive organisational news like new products or solutions, mergers, acquisitions, etc. On top of this, there could be more targeted sharing of thought leadership from the organisation aimed at relevant individuals. Perhaps news on the organisation's attempts to develop a blockchain solution is shared with the former tech employees, for example. There should also be invitations and details on events the company is running, both as normal day-to-business activities and also alumni-specific events. Finally, you could add a monthly communication asking for referrals for open positions. This list is, of course, by no means final. You are only limited by your imagination as to how far you can take the concept, and the best really push the envelope and expand the concept far and wide.

*If this book has brought you significant value, please share it with someone else who you feel could benefit from it. Thanks in advance!

Printed in Great Britain
by Amazon

10696060R00149